CARE OF

CARE OF

Letters, Connections,
and Cures

IVAN COYOTE

McClelland & Stewart

McClelland & Stewart and colophon are registered trademarks of
Penguin Random House Canada Limited.

Library and Archives Canada Cataloguing in Publication

Title: Care of / Ivan Coyote. Other titles: Care of (2021)
Names: Container of (work): Coyote, Ivan, 1969- Correspondence. Selections.
Description: Collection of correspondence written to and by Ivan Coyote.
Identifiers: Canadiana (print) 20200391798 | Canadiana (ebook) 20200392387 |
ISBN 9780771051722 (hardcover) | ISBN 9780771051739 (EPUB)
Subjects: LCSH: Coyote, Ivan, 1969-—Correspondence. |
CSH: Authors, Canadian (English)—21st century—Correspondence. |
LCSH: Storytellers—Canada—Correspondence. | LCGFT: Personal correspondence.
Classification: LCC PS8555.O99 Z48 2021 | DDC C813/.6—dc23

Lyrics on pages 79-80 from "Proud Crowd"
© Nemesis Publishing. Reproduced with permission from Ferron.

Lyrics on page 131 from "Mercy Now" by Mary Gauthier
© 2005 Mary Gauthier Songs. ALL RIGHTS RESERVED.

Book design by Kate Sinclair
Jacket art: Ivan Coyote
Typeset in Portrait by M&S, Toronto
Printed in the United States of America

McClelland & Stewart,
a division of Penguin Random House Canada Limited,
a Penguin Random House Company
www.penguinrandomhouse.ca

2nd Printing

Penguin
Random House
McCLELLAND & STEWART

This book is dedicated to every person who ever took the time to write me a special letter, whether delivered to me by snail mail, a hand-passed note, a text, a direct message or an email. I keep and remember them all.

TABLE OF CONTENTS

INTRODUCTION

I've been a road dog all of my adult life. My very first vehicle was a camper van, and I still miss it. Even before I became a touring writer and storyteller, I was a professional suitcase packer, a world-class map reader, a finely-tuned leaving machine. I wear through the soles of new boots ten times faster than I do bedsheets. Travel has been the spine and skeleton of my career for coming up on thirty years now. The two things all of my bones know best is telling stories on a stage, and the feeling of wheels or wings and road rolling under me.

Everybody on this continent remembers the week it all stopped. That weird week in mid-March of 2020 where the news about the virus wasn't coming from somewhere far away anymore, suddenly it was coming from our own hospitals, our own mouths, we were all breathing on each other still, and we needed to stop.

I was on the road when it happened. I had just finished a tour of high schools and libraries on Vancouver Island in the waning days of February, back when we were watching the news in China and Europe with one eye and washing our hands more often, but pretty much doing all other business as grinding and crowded as usual. In early March I had skipped up to the Yukon for three days to film a documentary, and then flown to Ontario. I was at my partner Sarah's place in London, Ontario, for a quick two-day visit before heading to St. Catharine's for a couple of gigs at Brock University.

I got a text at 9:45 p.m. on Thursday March 12th that both of my shows the next day had been cancelled. Luck and circumstance found me under Sarah's roof that night, not in a hotel room, and I am still grateful for that. By the following Monday most of the red dots on the next three months of my calendar had evaporated, along with all of my plans, and my main source of income. Sarah is a songwriter and touring musician, and we found ourselves sitting on the couch next to each other, answering emails and making a long grocery list with a lead-flavoured knot growing in both of our bellies.

Both of us had spent the better part of our best years practising the craft of, buying the gear for, and logging the hours in to becoming the very best live performers we could be, and overnight, all of our talents had been rendered irrelevant in this global pandemic landscape.

We did what everyone else we knew was doing. We bought a bag of rice, and canned beans, and counted how many rolls of toilet paper we had left. We watched the numbers tick upwards on the news, and we disinfected our groceries with our dwindling Lysol wipes. We told ourselves over and over how lucky we were to have a little money saved up, to have each other, to still be healthy. We will make the best of this time off of the road, we said. I can write some new songs, she said. I can work on my mystery novel, I said.

Except I couldn't. The story I was working on flips back and forth between 1986, where a small-town 19-year-old local boy goes missing from a bar one Friday night, and the present day, when his remains are finally discovered in the bush by a dog walker, just shy of 35 years after he disappeared.

I was in the groove for the 1986 parts, I was listening to "Jump" and "Born in the U.S.A." and "When Doves Cry" on repeat for inspiration, and it was working, but my words froze in my head when I tried to write about this present day. I spent hours staring at the flashing cursor on my computer screen. I made chili. I skipped rope outside in the carport because the gyms were closed. I cleared out a corner of Sarah's second bedroom and bought a little desk so I had my own place to work. Still. Imagining a world in this unimaginable time and place was impossible. Who could write fiction at a time like this?

So, I started answering my mail. I get a lot of mail. Emails, Twitter, Facebook and Instagram messages. Handwritten letters passed to me at the book signing table at a festival, a rain-soaked and blurry blue-inked note scrawled on the back of a flyer and left under the windshield of my car after a gig two years ago. Since 2009 or so I have been keeping both an electronic and a hard copy file of special letters, ones I always meant to sit down and answer properly, if and when I had the time. If and when was now upon me, and so I did.

This book does not answer all of my mail, not even close. I still owe so many beautiful writers a response to their missives. What I did was follow my storyteller's heart, and I chose the letter that most called out for an answer on the morning of each day I sat down to write.

Some of my replies stretched out into four or five pages. I answered each letter with a story that the original letter shook loose from my ribcage. Outside my office window the snow melted and the green fingers of the garden started to burst out of the dirt in the backyard. I had the time and the stillness to watch the ants crawl over the peony buds and learn the names of the birds arriving and departing the feeder we hung from the spruce tree. I had time to drink a second coffee in my bare feet. I had time to write letters.

By summer solstice all of those letters, and the stories and souls and substance they contained, were beginning to gather themselves into a much bigger conversation. Themes began to emerge. The longing of an older lesbian to be seen and remembered was answered and echoed by the call of a much younger queer writing to me in search of an elder. A letter from a lonely daughter found itself on my desk in the company of words from a proud and fearful father of a recently out trans son. Ex-evangelicals and the excommunicated were both communing in my email inbox, waiting for an answer. Some of the letters I wrote took me days to compose, and tinker with and tweak. I took deep breaths and long showers, and even longer walks. I wanted my replies to these letters to be perfect, especially the ones that I had been keeping safe for five or eight or even eleven years before crafting the kind of answers that they so deserved.

By the time September waned and became October, and it was time to prune back the faded green stalks of summer and get the garden ready for the snow to return, the much anticipated yet still somehow shocking second wave struck the world. I was afraid, but not like I had been in April. The unimaginable was now strangely familiar. I found myself always tired, even though I had much more time to sleep.

By this time those letters and my responses had merged themselves into the manuscript for this book. I started the process of contacting all of the letter writers by phone or text or email or Zoom, to ask them if they would consent to their letter to me being included in this now very extended and intentional conversation. A conversation with a remarkable collection of writers about family, and memory, and addiction, and loss, and joy, and forgiveness. A long conversation made possible by the simple and profound power of having the time to listen to each other.

None of the letters I received would have been addressed to me if I wasn't a traveller, a storyteller, a writer-downer of things and people I've met, and places I've been. Stories and the stage have in some way brought all of the beautiful people you are about to meet in these pages into my life. But most of the responses I wrote back to them would never have come out of me if the world hadn't forced most of us to stop and stay in one place for these last long and lonely months.

Those months, for me, were made far less lonely by the process of connecting and conversing with the twenty people who kindly agreed to include bits of their own lives and truths in this book. These letters, and the people who wrote them, were a lifeline for me, an antidote, a cure for the sudden stillness of the wheels under me. Our stories can still travel, I tell myself every morning, watching the weeks wax and then wane through our kitchen window. I now know the names of most of my neighbours in this place I never meant to be in for long.

In early December I took a walk around the marsh and pond across the road from where I have been living. All summer that pond and the marsh that surrounds it were jumping and croaking with frogs and toads of many varieties. In early winter though, it was quiet enough for me to hear the frost crystals as they crunched under my winter boots, and I got to wondering where frogs go to escape the cold. Years ago, I would have just pondered this mystery until I got home and could look it up, but that day I simply sat down in the forest on the little bench where the two paths split, on the hill after the boardwalk ends, and I googled it on my phone.

I learned that some frogs hibernate under the ice, suspended in the frigid water, absorbing the very little bit of oxygen they need by breathing through their permeable skins. Toads must dig themselves deep into the soil, sometimes over 50 centimetres down, to get below the frost line and escape the winter freeze. A few species of frogs have found another way. They have become freeze tolerant. They hide away in dead leaves or under bark, and tiny ice crystals form in their frog bodies, freezing about 40 per cent of the water content inside of them. The frog ceases to breathe, its blood does not flow and its heart stops beating. It cheats the cold by becoming it. In the spring it thaws out when the temperature rises and hops away.

I'm still not sure what kind of an amphibian I would be, but I do think of all of those kinds of frogs as I watch the snow fall and drag another bag of rice from my car to the pantry and wait for a vaccine to make it into my own lonesome and homesick veins.

It is early January as I write this. The sidewalks here are slippery with a skiff of snow that fell this morning over the ice that gathered there last night. Spring seems still so far from this place. It feels too soon yet for me to dare imagine the world that the printed copy of this book will be released into.

I sincerely hope that by the time anyone is able to remove this book from a shelf and open these pages and begin to read them, that we will all be able to gather safely together again to thaw ourselves out, to stretch, to blink, to hug each other hard, and to listen to us all tell stories.

In the meantime, please write me a letter.

I.

ALL OF MY OTHER UNCLES

DECEMBER 12, 2019

Hi my name is Ace, I was the older guy with the walker sitting in the front row lipreading you last night. I really enjoyed your performance. I am a binary transgender man, and lately I have received a lot of boomer and binary bashing from my trans brothers, as well as assumptions from women about all men being misogynist and because I am now a man, I feel the pain of that deeply. After fifteen years of testosterone's effects I cannot cry. My soul is non-binary, but I needed to be physically binary. I know that you accept everyone's choice concerning their body politics and as a feminist and former lesbian, so do I. I wanted to know if the binary trans man will ever be seen as anything other than a sell out to the gender binary. I would love the gender divide between the genders to disappear. Your story about AIDS hurting the community in the early 80s touched me deeply. I lost many friends to AIDS at that time. I just beat cancer, and struggle with nerve and muscle pain. I am almost 60 and I was hoping that you could help me understand the backlash that I am getting from my non-binary brothers in the younger trans-gender population. I am disabled and hard of hearing but I want to think that I have value in the community. Any thoughts on how we can stop the divide between binary and non-binary individuals.

Thank you,
Ace.

Dear Ace:

Your words have been rattling around in my heart for 35 days now. Your questions slip up and tap me on the shoulder while I'm standing undressed and alone in a long shower, and I can still see you, leaning forward in the first seat in the front row—lately the shape of you is often the last thing I see at night when I close my eyes to sleep.

I met a full-grown adult human that same night at the theatre, a bill-paying, driver's license–bearing, legally-drinking citizen who was born in the year 2000, can you imagine that? I'm fifty years old now and the sound of those words still seem impossible to say, but my tongue keeps making the truth out of them.

I talk to youth all of the time, but most days I feel more like a historian than any kind of leader. I must be way too young to be an elder, but still, I'm often the oldest person in the room. The prime minister is younger than I am. Recently, often so is the principal of the high school I have been invited to speak at.

Strangers in restaurants and airports and liquor stores don't mistake me for a teenage boy so much anymore. These hips. These hips don't fit any of the words I use to describe myself, these hips don't fit the space shaped like me I hold inside of my head, and I don't have any of the answers you asked me for.

Some days I feel something that might look like a strategy or a manifesto or a plan start to shimmer and form inside of me, the words line up into almost ideas and then scatter, and evaporate. What began as clear becomes fear. I think I first heard the words non-binary about eight or nine years ago. It's a term that mostly belongs to people younger than me. That in itself makes me old. Saying anything new when you are old is a new thing for me. Non-binary. The term sticks to me just a little bit better than the word woman ever did, and it settles itself over both of my shoulders without slipping off as much as the word trans always tends to do. There are never enough words to describe all of all of us, though, are there? How could one word hold both of us inside of it?

So, I will just tell you that I looked out that snowy Tuesday night last month and I saw you sitting right there in the front row, and you looked like family to me. Like an uncle, like a brother. We are more *us* than you will ever be *them* to me. You tell me fifteen years of testosterone took your tears away from you, but don't worry, I've still got more than enough for both of us.

I'm so glad the cancer didn't get you. I'm grateful that you braved the pain on such an icy night and we got a chance to meet. Do you speak sign language, or would captioning the event have helped you more? Thank you for reminding me that inaccessible venues and events keep so many of us away, and that I need to do so much more for you. Maybe you wouldn't doubt your value to the community if we showed it to you more often.

I want you to know I love the grey in your beard and how your slim wrists turn into hairy arms and your honey-over-gravel voice and your belt and suspenders. I'm sorry so many of our siblings don't or can't or won't see our shared history. But I remember. You are our secret weapon, our double agent, our man on the inside. We are all so much more than the outside of ourselves, and I know that you know this more than most of us ever could. I know we both carry the ghosts of what we lived through with us still, I know we can't forget what they called us, and what we have discarded, what we won and have lost, and what it cost us.

I know that the difference between coming out in 1979 and 1989 cannot just be called ten years. I know I'm standing on so many older shoulders even now as I write this.

My work these days is taking everything I know about masculinity and turning it over, and then over again, and deciding what to keep and what must be discarded now, to check myself and change myself so I am not standing even accidentally in the way of all women and girls moving into their rightful power and place in this world. I believe the balance and future of this planet depends on this. This does not mean I don't want you with me, or that you are not needed. I imagine you there right beside me when we dismantle it all. All of us will be necessary, and none of us are disposable.

I remember meeting a trans woman in Edmonton. It was thirteen years ago, and she was in her seventies, I think. She told a whole room of queer youth that if they were trans, they should go on hormones and get surgery as soon as they legally could. She said the only way to survive as a trans person was to try to pass as your (her words) target gender as much as was possible, that living in between the binary was simply too hard, and very few could do it. At the time I could not comprehend how she could say those things, especially with in-between me standing right next to her, about to speak to the very same youth right after her. I didn't understand her thirteen years ago, but today I can sit here and see her a little better. She had been a schoolteacher, fired from her job for transitioning in Edmonton in the eighties, way before any hormones or surgery were covered by health care.

I'm starting to see that it is not my place to ponder what she felt her options were back then, or what decisions she might have made thirty or forty years into this future. I think my opinion on her means of survival back then is beyond irrelevant now. I know that my real job is to listen and believe, and honour and remember, and continue to fight and to write. Write it all down.

Maybe the point of writing it all down is not necessarily just so the next generations will find these words and read them and be convinced of anything, other than the fact that I existed. Maybe when I am dust I will have let go of this need to explain anything, or be understood by anyone. Maybe it will be enough to just not be forgotten altogether.

I think there is a reason for the divide between generations. I think these kids need to reinvent the possibilities for themselves, and in order to do that they have to, for a while at least, forget us, and our pain. They need to learn on their own to spit back much of what we had to swallow. They need to never know all the things that stood in our way. They need to take what we fought for and won for granted, so they can make room to expect so much more than we dared to ever hope about. Then we can all inherit new language, more words, a better day.

In the meantime, I will not forget you, or her, or myself. And, for as long as I am able, I will write.

2.

YOUR KATE

Hello Ivan:

It has taken me a very long time to find the strength and courage to reach out to you. I hope it is alright, I just have some things that have been weighing on me that I need to say to you. I saw you speak at the BC Federation of Labour convention in November 2018, and I so regret that I didn't have the chance to speak with you then, but I found myself so overcome with emotion that I could only sit sobbing in my seat. In April of that year I lost my 21-year-old daughter to suicide. She was my world, and I was still grieving and coming to grips with what had happened. She began her transition when she was 17, and completed her physical transition the December before she passed. We had many many talks about her struggles and pain that she was going through over the years, and although I loved her fully and completely, I never could fully put myself in her shoes. She struggled to share some basic experiences that she went through because I will admit, I became fiercely protective of her, but also, she didn't want to see me hurt because she was in pain. That day as I listened to you speak, it was like I was hearing the words that she wanted me to hear. You spoke directly to my heart, and I was finally able to understand the struggles and hurt that she must have gone through just in day-to-day life. And for that I need to say thank you. I appreciate so much that you were there when I needed those words, even if you didn't know the huge effect that it would have on someone in the group.

I hope this doesn't come across as some crazed fan, lol. I am coming to see you speak in Nanaimo in a few weeks, and if some short reddish-haired person tries to shake your hand but can't form words to speak to you that will be me, and I hope you will just shake my hand and remember the words I have said here.

Thank you for your time,
Adri

This is a picture of my Kate

APRIL 3, 2020

Dear Adri:

First of all, please let me start off by offering you my condolences, what-ever that might actually mean to a mother who has lost her child. I offer you my sincere condolences. My sympathy. I offer my pledge to you that I will continue to share my own stories, so that they might manage to continue to find their way to you, and bring you even the tiniest comfort.

I'm so grateful to receive these words from you, and I am honoured that you have trusted me with the small window that these letters offer me into your story, and your life, and your grief. I promise to choose my next words carefully, and with all of the compassion and tenderness my own heart is capable of.

Thank you for sending me that picture of your daughter Kate. She was a beautiful young woman. She reminds me a little of my niece (well, technically Layla would be my second cousin, she's my cousin Dan's daughter, but in my family, she is called my niece). In fact, I think there is even a photo out there somewhere of Layla with the very same hot pink streaks in her jet-black hair, the same perfect black eyeliner and mascara as Kate wore in that picture, the same leather collar and chains, and nearly the same nose piercing. I bet if they had ever met, they would have drunk strong coffee with too much milk and sugar in it, and exchanged sarcastic jokes while giving less cool passers-by immaculate side-eye between careful sips so as not to ruin their perfect lipliner.

I'm glad you and I got to shake hands at my gig last month, even though I didn't realize at the time that you were the woman who wrote me this letter. I've put all the pieces together now. That was a special gig, that night at the library in Nanaimo. So many queer and trans people were there, like the non-binary kid in grade nine at the local high school, with their mom and stepdad in tow, all the old butches with their wallet chains and hiking boots and their reading glasses tucked into plaid shirt pockets. The femmes with their purses hooked on the backs of their chairs. My mom's friend Rona was there too, and Ivan the old guitar player from the Yukon, and the library regulars, and that woman doing her knitting in the first row. Did you see the old man who offered me his handkerchief at the end there? A white, folded and pressed hankie, the kind that you buy in boxes of three in the menswear department at the Bay. My friend Shelagh from the CBC radio.

Every gig is different, but I admit that I most love the shows where there is no fee for the members of the audience. The library covered my wage that night, so it meant that I got paid, and everyone could be there in that room, they even had special accessible parking and seating, and I printed up hard copies of my script for my friends who are hard of hearing.

Some nights I really get to feel like I am speaking to all of the people, and February 26, 2020 at the Nanaimo North branch of the Vancouver Island Regional Library was definitely one of them. Some nights you can see and feel and hear the stories doing the magic that only stories can do in a room full of listening hearts. It is a sacred thing, it is a blessed exchange, and I am always crumpled and humbled and healed afterwards.

Lately when I am about to get up on a stage I do this thing, just before I start. I imagine that there is a giant seam that runs from the centre of my collarbone, just at the base of my throat, straight down past my sternum, right down to about where my belt buckle sits. I imagine that my ribcage can be split open by that seam, that my heart and my guts are behind two double doors made out of my ribs, and just before I step on stage I open those doors all the way, so there is nothing hard or made of bone between my inside bits and the people I am about to speak to. This spills me and holds me all together at the same time, somehow, and allows me to step right into the insides of the story I am telling, my own heart pumping there in both of my open hands. If I do it right I can feel it, I can feel the story looping out of me and into you, leaving little bits of itself behind, and then sailing back into me, still familiar but not the same anymore, somehow, grown bigger now and carrying tiny parts of every heart in the room along with it.

I can never sleep when I crawl into whatever rented or borrowed bed I end up in after, exhausted and elated. Believe me when I say that I still hold a little sliver of your grief inside of me, it lives now in the bones in my back, and it comes and sits some days on my shoulders, and reminds me why. It's why I recognized your daughter in that picture you sent me, even though I don't think I ever got to meet her. I carry her with me, and I remember. Her story reached in and rattled the ghosts that remain in me.

His name was Christopher. My aunt Roberta's oldest son. My mom's nephew. My awkward and gangly cousin. I was the oldest of my generation, and I was supposed to protect him but could not. I could not shield him from the cruelty of children, or stand in front of the fists or tongue of his stepfather. In the end I could not save him from himself. He was also 21.

I don't in any way liken my loss to that of his mother's. But I do still rent a room in my chest full of the regret and rage and love and guilt and what ifs that suicide leaves inside those it leaves behind, and I have come to realize after 26 years that this room in me will always be occupied. I cannot empty it. I am unable to lose the key.

Storytellers are not meant to forget these things. We are tasked with saving them.

I was raised Catholic. There are too many cruel things about my discarded faith to include in one letter, or one lifetime, not the least of which is what Catholicism preaches to its believers about queer and trans people. People like Christopher, and your Kate, and myself.

One thing I will never forgive the Catholics for is telling my aunt Roberta that Christopher's soul is not welcome now in heaven. That his remains cannot be held in consecrated earth. I believe in no god that would ever burden a mother with such blasphemy. I don't know where Christopher's spirit lives most of the time, but I do know this: he stands just to one side and right behind me every time I speak to high school kids and tell them that they are blessed, and holy, and sacred, no matter who they love or who they are. I can feel him standing there, and I know he is smiling.

Thank you for writing to me, Adri. Thank you for shaking my hand in Nanaimo. I promise you I will never forget your words. They have their own little room inside of me now, and the fire is warm. You and Kate are always welcome to meet me there. I will leave the light on for you.

With much love,
Ivan

3.

OUR FATHERS

NOVEMBER 4, 2019

Greetings, Ivan.

Where I am in your new book is the chapter called "Twelve: Remember that Song?". I had planned to wait until I finished it completely before writing to you, but I'm pretty excited about it, and maybe writing to you while I'm still reading it is a way of prolonging the whole experience.

I'm basically inhaling every word and when I go back to immediately begin re-reading it, I'll be surprised if there's anything left on the page. It's been a very rough few years for me, so my usual solace of incessant reading hasn't been there. Couldn't focus.

Your book is bringing reading back to life for me at the moment and I'm pretty grateful for that. Also, it's making me laugh, which is always a good thing.

I love that you mention Tom Spanbauer. He wrote one of my favourite books (*I Loved You More*). I'd say I'm obsessed with masculinity, though I still can't define what the hell it is. And that book stands out to me as a gorgeous rendering of masculinity. I was transported when I read it.

I grew up in Saskatoon, so your Moose Jaw experience takes me back to the continuous violence I experienced growing up in Saskatchewan in the 60s and 70s.

Had to get the hell out of there, and am glad I survived it to get to Toronto at 19—even though I forever miss the flat land and seeing rain miles away and the northern lights and the sun dogs and the dry air and Cranberry Flats.

I never felt safe there either; never do in small cities or towns. My partner and I drove the Cabot Trail one summer and stopped in Mabou. I got totally triggered and someone shouted at me out of a truck and I couldn't stop being scared that I'd be dragged behind the pub we were in and, well, you know exactly what I was scared of.

My friend lives in the Yukon and after my mother died in 1994 I drove solo from Saskatoon to Mile 1053 on the Alaska Highway. That was gorgeous and my friend lived on Kluane Lake then in a cabin with a permafrost pit in the back for a fridge. I've known her since we were both 4.

Last night I went with my partner and 4-year-old son to a dinner at a rented venue. It was a family event, a baptism celebration for her nephew. I was walking to the bathroom when the person in the coat check informed me that I could not use the Women's . . . I did tell her a couple of times that I wasn't a man, but by the time I was washing my hands, she had summoned another staff member who came in and said, "Sir, you can NOT be in here." I told her the same thing and then there was the usual awkwardness and embarrassment on her part. The kind where you actually start feeling bad for the other person and even lean toward apologizing but stop short of it.

Then I went back to the table where I already felt pretty out of place in my suspenders and dress pants and boots. And I remembered all the times my bladder's nearly burst because it isn't safe.

When it happened the day before at the Y, it was an older naked woman and she looked really scared and I was able to find the humour in it all.

But last night I couldn't and I had you and your book on my mind. So I just went to Facebook and looked at your photos and that helped a lot.

Then I read more of your book when I got home and tried not to read too fast so I could savour it. And that helped too.

I hope you don't mind that I'm attaching a not very long piece that I wrote several years ago about my relationship with my dad. I say I hope you don't mind because people probably inundate you with this sort of thing—and I'm not asking you to do anything but read it. Sending because there's so much I relate to in you, so much cross-over between us.

It's taken me this long to actually send you an email. Since *Boys Like Her*—that's when I first "met" you. 1998.

Thank you for your lovely comment on my Facebook post about your book; I'm quite sure it opened the door for me to communicate with you in this way.

I don't know how to thank you for all the other stuff you've done for me with your writing, your shows, your interviews, video clips, and your existence. But I think you're a beauty and it's a great solace to me to have you as a touchstone in this gawdfersakin world.

Love to you, Ivan.
fogel

Dear fogel:

When I first got your email, I flagged it in my Gmail with the little red flag button, on my phone. I remember where I was when I read it the first time. Just home from the road, and sitting in my car outside of the Vancouver airport waiting for Sarah, my partner, to appear outside of the arrivals door. We had a big show two days later, and we drove straight from the airport to the rehearsal space to practice with the band. Didn't even go home.

This is one of those letters, I thought to myself. It will take a while to properly answer this one. Put it in the special file. And so I did. That was five months ago come this Sunday. It's a Friday night in April of the year 2020. Outside most of the world's doors a virus is replicating and looking for hosts. Behind some of those doors that virus is weakening lungs and stealing the lives of the loved and the lonely alike. Everything has changed. I'm not on the road anymore, and no one knows when it will be safe again to gather together to tell and listen to stories. So I'm finally answering all those special letters.

First of all, I'm sorry to hear that the last few years have been rough ones for you. It's weird, with you and I—I feel like I've known you for years, from fleeting meetings before or after gigs, and from social media messages and posts, but we've never had a drink together, or even sat at a table with two coffees steaming between us. Still I feel like I've known you for a long time. I think we first met in 1998 or so, does that sound right? I think we're around the same age, maybe you are a couple of years older than me, but not much. It's not just the butch (plus?) thing, either—I mean, it is that, but it's more than that, too. I have always known you didn't grow up in a big city, even though I've only ever seen you in Toronto. I recognize the neighbour in you, the elementary school you could walk to, the corner store where you would buy those gummies shaped like Coke bottles, and Fudgsicles and sour candies with change you made from collecting pop bottles and babysitting and mowing lawns. If I lived in Saskatoon growing up in the 70s we would have ridden our red five-speeds around the subdivision together under all that sky until the summer sun made long shadows on the dusty chip seal in front of our tires.

We are starting to get old together. Our hair is greying at roughly the same pace. My barber would know exactly how to cut your hair, and yours would mine. We probably own a couple of the same blue shirts. Are your Blundstones black, or brown, or do you own two pairs, like I do? I don't know the name your father gave you, or if I ever did I forgot it decades ago, and you never knew the name my father still slips and calls me sometimes, and you and I, we both like it that way.

Those old names don't apply anymore, and in most ways they never really did.

I just read your piece about your father a second time. I'm in Ontario, like you, about two hours away from the city, in London. It's Tuesday, April 7 now, around 10 p.m. Outside a huge storm is raging, flashes of lightning blind the sky over the townhouse complex where my girlfriend lives, lighting up and then disappearing the roofs and windows of the neighbours every 30 seconds or so, and the thunder sounds almost right on top of the bolts of light. I let myself imagine for a long second or two that this storm can wash away a virus, that after the weather moves on and the sky clears tomorrow morning this will all be over, and we can open our doors again, invite each other in. Sit at the same table and share the same food. Play music with each other and sing and tell stories. Share the same glass of whiskey.

I'm willing myself to keep writing. It is the thing I can do best, it is nearly the only thing about this life that still makes me feel connected, other than kissing Sarah, and feeling the dog asleep near my feet on the bed before the alarm goes off and reminds me of the world right now.

My phone makes a newsflash sound. *Beep beep beep beep.* Another bulletin. John Prine has just died. Now the rain is running down my face. John Prine was 73 years old. Same age as my father.

Your father was a doctor. He was graceful and slim and a good dancer, you wrote. Mine was a welder. My father does not have beautiful hands. His are wide and so scarred all over from all those burns that he can pull the roast chicken pan quickly out of the oven bare-handed and drop it on the top of the stove without further blistering his perpetually work-blackened palms and fingertips. There is nearly nothing graceful about him, except for how straight a bead he can draw with a welding torch in molten steel or aluminum.

They have almost nothing in common, your father and mine, save for the fact that they both have man daughters, and both of them tell both of us that they are ready to die now.

The first time my father talked about dying was right after the divorce. He was drunk and living in a little squatter's house he built behind his rented shop. He told me that if he ever got so sick that he needed to piss or shit into a bag like his friend Willy did now that he wanted me to take that old elephant gun that he had inherited from his uncle John Francis and shoot him in the head with it.

"You'd do that for me, right? Put me out of that kind of misery?"

It was a test I knew I was going to fail before he even finished his sentence.

"No, Dad, I will not shoot you in the head. Not with that gun anyways. It's an antique revolver last fired in the Boer War. It would blow up in my face and I'd spend the rest of my life in jail with an eye patch. Be realistic. Pick a better method, or at least a more reliable gun."

He squints at me from his easy chair. Swirls what is left of the scotch on the rocks in his glass. Swallows it. Gets up to put another log on the fire. Doesn't speak to me again for about 15 minutes, and when he does it is about other things.

I was about 30 years old then, and he was fifty-two. Pretty much the same age as I am now. He seemed old then already. I have to get up and stretch before I can write anymore tonight because my back has been sore today.

At 6 a.m. on the morning of November 29, 2016, my cell phone woke me up. I was in a motel room in Duncan, a small pulp mill town on Vancouver Island, on my last day of touring my new book.

The display on my phone told me my Uncle Fred was calling me. My Uncle Fred had never called me in my entire life. I only had his number saved in my phone because I text him on his birthday, and call him whenever I need to ask for advice about mechanical stuff. He's a heavy equipment mechanic. They call him an engine whisperer. Legend has it he can hear or sometimes smell what is wrong with a motor without lifting a wrench. He tilts his head like the conductor of an orchestra, listening, with one forefinger raised, waiting for the engine to whine or cry out about what is troubling it.

I answer the phone, because I know it has to be an emergency. It is.

My father has attempted suicide, Fred tells me. He doesn't know any details, and him and my Uncle Rob are driving out to Atlin to find out what is going on. They are just about at the cut-off, and about to lose cell service, but he will call me in about three or four hours when they can get back in cell range and let me know. Fred doesn't even know if my dad is dead, or if they were able to resuscitate him at the little nurse's station in Atlin. He will call me as soon as he can, he promises. Thought you should know, he says, and then his voice breaks up, and the signal drops and he is gone.

I had to go and teach a writing workshop to a group made up of about thirty women who were living in a transition home, and a gaggle of teenage girls in plaid-skirted private school uniforms, because life is weird and waits for no one's tragedies to pass, and by the time the catered box lunches arrived my uncle had called me back. My dad was alive, and in an ambulance, and on his way to the hospital in Whitehorse, where he would be treated for his wounds, and then admitted to the psych ward for assessment.

Your dad was right, knives are messy, and self-inflicted knife wounds are unreliable. When he woke up still alive, and still drunk, my dad peeled the dried and bloodied sheets from his clothes and stumbled outside to the garage and locked himself in with the doors all closed, started up his pickup, rolled all the windows down and waited.

But his friend Lance woke up long before sunrise that morning with a bad feeling in the corners of his guts. So, he got up, threw on his sheepskin-lined jean jacket and drove his big truck down the little dirt road that runs between his fancy house on the lake and my dad's humble home in the pine trees, to go and check on him. At first, he just drove past and nearly turned around and went home. My dad's truck wasn't parked outside where it usually was. Lance thought maybe my dad had just got up really early and gone into town. Thought maybe he'd just check on the house, since my dad had been pretty drunk the night before. Make sure it was all locked up okay.

First thing wrong was Buddy was still in the house, barking and whining behind the unlocked door. My dad never went to town without taking the dog. Then Lance saw the blood on the kitchen floor. He knocked, then froze, listening. Heard the truck running from inside the garage, and he knew.

Lance shouldered the door to the garage open and fell inside, falling to the concrete floor and cracking his elbow up pretty bad. Pulled my unconscious father out of his truck and onto the gravel outside of the garage door, and limped inside to call Dolores the nurse on the landline. Lance was over seventy at the time, and he had both of his feet crushed in a car accident years ago, and they still hurt him real bad, especially in the cold, and he often bragged about the scar on his ass and leg from a grizzly bear attack. He wore a tooth that he pulled out of that bear's mouth after he shot it on a chain around his neck, with a gold nugget he mined himself embedded in it, just so you get a picture in your head of who Lance was. He died of a heart attack last summer, outlived by the guy whose life he saved that day.

That was nearly four years ago. If I was making any of this story up, I would give it a better ending than it has right now. If any of this were fiction Lance would still be with us, and my Dad would be clean and sober now, and doing little welding jobs for folks in town to keep a little money coming in on top of his government pension and planning what to plant in his garden this spring. If I could write my father a better life story, his second wife would have won her battle with that brain tumour back in 2013, and everything might be different now.

I just read the story about your father for the third time. You're a great writer. Really. It's a tough but beautiful piece of work. I can't tell at the end if your father is still alive, if he still sort of knows you, or what he remembers.

My dad has memory loss due to alcoholism, it's a syndrome, but I don't recall the name for it now and I don't use it, because it is named after the surname of the scientist who discovered it, and I truly feel like my father has invented his very own personal version of this affliction. It's hard to tell what he can't remember anymore, what he was drunk when he first learned, and thus has now forgotten, or what he simply didn't care about in the first place, and so wasn't listening to when you told him the first time around.

I just read that last paragraph back three times and considered deleting it. I don't want to give you the idea that I do not love my father. Some days I wish I could make myself love him less than I do. If I didn't love him it would hurt us both less, I think. I look a lot like him, especially in pictures when I am smiling, or looking down at something I'm holding in my hands.

When he is sober he is so funny, and charming. When I was a kid he could draw nearly anything, without ever erasing a line and starting over, like the picture was already there on the blank paper and all he had to do was reveal it with the tip of his pencil. He used to design and build boats. He could weld and fix anything. He built both of the houses we lived in growing up with his own hands, from sketches on napkins and on the backs of telephone or electric bills. He taught me to weld and drive a truck and trailer and a forklift and saw a perfect 90 on a two-by-four and cook a perfect pancake. He built the little house he still lives in today, too, for his late wife Patricia. A little two-bedroom in Atlin, a little town about two hours south of Whitehorse. They moved there full-time when she retired from the auto parts place, about six months before she found that lump in her neck and asked him to drive her back into town to see the doctor about it. She was going to ask him about the headaches, too, while she was at it.

I still know everything he taught me about the world of men and the things men of his class and age are expected to know how to do, and I am grateful for most of it. It was unusual to have your ten-year-old daughter in oversized greasy coveralls sweeping and sorting bolts in your shop in 1979, but he did it. Maybe because he knew I could and that I liked it, or maybe because of his lack of a son to bring to work instead of me. I still love the smell of that orange-scented mechanic's hand cleanser. Lanolin. I still love the ozone smell in the air when someone is arc welding, and when the Skilsaw blade gets a bit dull and scorches the plywood on long cuts.

I am nearly fifty-one and still dismantling most of what I learned from him about masculinity. Trying to build the salvageable bits into something that might better serve the kind of world I want to exist in. One thing I have always loved about my father is his ability to cry. He cries at stories, at sad songs. He cries when a bird flies into the window or he drives past a road-killed deer. He cries for shame and regret and the people and things he has lost. I inherited his easy tears, and I am working on trying to shed the urge to apologize for those tears that I also learned from him.

My mother is the stoic one. The one you depend on, the one you call in an emergency. The one I don't need to take care of as much, not yet.

I should stop now before this letter turns into a novella.

Thank you for taking my call last night. I was typing this letter, and stopped to check my Facebook, and you had just commented on that silly video I posted. So, I just clicked once on your profile, and then again on the little phone icon, and there you were. I read you your letter to me first, as it has been months since you sent it to me, and then I read you my response, as much as had gotten done so far. I couldn't tell if you cried but I did. I've never done anything like that before, and I'm not

sure why I called you, but I'm glad we got to talk. We finally sort of had that virtual coffee, 22 years after we first met. I told you I would call you back and read you the rest, and I will. I know we still have so much to talk about. Thank you again for your letter, and this connection that it has brought us, and I sincerely look forward to the friendship that I know will unfold from here. I have always seen the sibling in you, the family resemblance.

Happy Passover, fogel. It brings me great comfort to know you get to spend it with your partner, and your son. I hope to meet them both when we are on the other side of this.

Talk to you soon.

Much love and solidarity,
Ivan

4.

SHINY-SHOED STORYTELLER

Ivan,

I'll start with a secret, something I feel slightly guilty about. I had full intention of inviting my entire cohort of student teachers here tonight. It was the perfect opportunity for some of my peers to see that it's not only me who uses these pronouns. That it's not only me with these stories to tell. Two weeks ago I was going to send around an email. Last week I was going to mention it in class. Yesterday, I was going to remind a few key folks about it . . . I did none of those things. Rather than enlighten others to your beautiful mind, I continued to keep my mouth shut.

After a particularly rough week, I wanted to keep you to myself a little while longer. To savour your strength and be embraced by your warmth and humour. I didn't want to discuss you/us the following day in class. I didn't want to share you.

I've been coming home a little more tired lately, frustrated by the constant misgendering. A few nights ago, I tucked into bed with your new book and a cuppa tea. I stayed up until 2 a.m. reading, feeling like we were processing that day together. Sharing you tonight meant sharing those intimate moments that are holding me together this year. It meant sharing my truths and shame to people who still fail to see me. During a time when so much of my self, my vulnerability, is on public display, I just couldn't bring myself to invite them.

But! Please know that next time I will. Know that every time you step on a school stage, I'm standing strong beside you. Proud to share community with you. Grateful for your vulnerability. Ready to catch you at any moment.

I constantly have students approach me in the hall or gym of my practicum school. Small comments like "your voice is squeaky" or "I'm confused by whether you're a boy or a girl" or "I like your haircut . . . I REALLY like your haircut." These moments are heartwarming. Said with such gentle curiosity, kids are making connections in a school that currently feels hostile to anything outside the ordinary. There are some really beautiful moments of being trans.

Anyway. I suppose I wanted to say that I hold so much love for these stories you share. Our stories.

Thank you,
Tem

P.S. When I first came out to my folks, I suggested that they go see your show in Victoria. They went and absolutely fell in love with you. My mum now follows you on Instagram (she's a big fan of your cabin building posts) and my dad asks how you are, like we're friends. I told him I'd check in with you this week. So, how are you?

Dear Tem:

First of all, thank you so much for coming to my show at the library. I wonder if I wish I knew at the time it would be my last public show before the pandemic hit, and we would be here, 10 weeks later, in this permanently changed world, hunkered down in our homes, if we are one of the lucky ones.

I think a lot now of those last few days before we knew what was going on. Imagine now, cramming over 200 people into a library in Nanaimo? That gig would not have happened at all if it had been scheduled even two weeks later. It wouldn't have happened if we had any idea of what was about to happen to the world we thought we knew.

I think of how many hugs I gave and received that night, and simultaneously feel grateful and terrified remembering each one of them.

Schools are closed still. Most teachers I know are scrambling right now, trying to adapt their physical classes and in-person lessons for students now sheltering at home with iPads and ADHD, and exhausted parents googling how to do grade 8 algebra while prepping dinner and Zooming with their co-workers. I'm not sure where the pandemic leaves you, a student teacher? How does one do a teaching practicum at a shuttered school?

I've been doing some form of my anti-bullying school show for 17 years now. I've performed for 2200 kids in a giant theatre in Auckland, New Zealand, and 400 uniformed and silent kids in a government school in Hong Kong. I've clocked thousands of kilometres alone in my truck, or rented cars, all over this continent, and on four others, too. I once made a hippie kid in a tiny mountain town near the BC-Alberta border laugh so hard he fell off of his chair in the library and peed his hand-me-down jeans just a little bit. His name was Rain, a detail I learned after the gig was over, from the librarian, and I laughed all the way down the highway back to my hotel room at that one.

I have a complicated relationship to school shows. It runs deep and thick, right through my veins and down into my marrow. I did a rough count last year, and I estimate that I've performed for over half a million kids now, give or take, a number which makes me feel proud and exhausted at the same time.

After each and every school show I've ever done, without exception, I've been approached by a kid. You're a student teacher so you know this kid already.

A kid with a question that isn't really a question at all. A kid with a little seedling of themselves wrapped up in the disguise of a question, and he or she or they hold it in there, in sweaty palms, and lift it into the space between us, and unwrap it just a little, just enough to let a bit of light leak onto it. Gymnasium floor beneath our feet and the smell of someone's armpits floating everywhere around us, and this kid shows me a little of who they are, in an immense and sacred act of untested trust.

"Why do you cut your hair so short? My mom won't let me. Yet."

"Your story about your grandmother reminded me so much of my grandma. Does she still love you?"

"What pronoun do you use?"

"Where is your cousin Christopher now, the one that got picked on in school so much?"

"Did you see my rainbow shoelaces? I got them at Walmart."

"Do you believe in unicorns? In Bigfoot?"

"Are you married?"

Sometimes they have turquoise hair and half of their head shorn close, and have already changed their names and told their mom but not their dad yet. Sometimes you can spot them from a mile away, in their skinny jeans and David Bowie tshirt.

But sometimes not. Sometimes he is the kid that bounces a basket-ball over in the corner all the way through sound check and asks no questions at all but stays in the gym until everyone else is gone and then follows me out to my car to tell me that he liked my show and that I should be a stand-up comedian. I stop and turn and face him, make space for him to say something else, but he doesn't. We both stand there next to the driver's door of my truck until it gets a little awkward, and we tell each other goodbye. He stands there with his bangs a little in his eyes and the ball sitting on one hip and his eyes full of things he wants to say but his mouth all dry and quiet. He watches me drive away, growing smaller in my rear-view until I turn the corner and he is gone. Sometimes he will write me an email that night, or the next day, but most times not. Still. I came to his school and stepped in front of everyone and spoke with my head up and my shoulders back and let the pride seep out of me and into the air we all shared, and maybe he breathed in even the smallest breath of some of it and kept it for him-self, for later.

I carry a little piece of each of those kids away with me, show after show, and town after town and sometimes I can't tell one school parking lot from another but I remember all of their faces, I do. My back aches from all that driving and my gas pedal foot seizes up sometimes when I walk across the tarmac from my truck to my hotel room after. I drop my backpack onto the other bed, and kick off my boots. Even a twenty-minute shower isn't long enough to ponder all of the stories I collected that day, I can scrub my shoulders until they glow red but the stories of those kids stick with me, and I carry them into the next day. They are not burdens, though, it's so much more complicated than just that. It's like finding a little stone in your pocket, or the bottom of your bag, or even in your shoe, but when you flip it over, you can see wings there, too, folded up now around the underside of the stone, but there still. And you wonder if this means that one day that stone will fly, or if it means that it once flew but has now forgotten how, but you must keep it, because it is a magic stone still, either way.

But pockets and backpacks and suitcases filled with even tiny stones add up.

In February and March of 2019, I was booked to do something like 40 school shows in a little over a month in Surrey. It was part of an initiative paid for by the school district to address bullying of queer and trans students. Usually when a school brings me in my fee is paid for by that school, or by the school's parent advisory committee, but for this tour my fees were all paid by the school board. It wasn't mandatory for a school to participate, and when I agreed to the project the school district said it would probably be about 15-20 schools that would sign up to bring me in to speak to their students.

Well, that is not what happened at all. All but two schools in the entire district responded, and some schools wanted me to do multiple shows, so that I could speak to all of the students in every grade in their school, and their gym would only hold 800 kids at a time.

I used to never have a cap on how many students I would speak to at one time, but I changed that a few years ago, after learning the very hard way that speaking to 1,100 kids at the same time in a giant gym in Fort St. John at 2 p.m. on a Friday afternoon in late spring before a long weekend is very bad for my physical and mental health. I made a new rule that I would only speak to a maximum of 600 kids at a time.

But I broke that rule in February of 2019. I told myself that all those queer and trans kids living in Surrey needed to be represented. I told myself I could do it. I told myself that I needed the money. I told myself that speaking to 800 kids wouldn't be that much harder than speaking to 600 kids. Eighty out of those eight hundred kids are queer or trans, I told myself, whether their parents or their parents' gods like it or not, those are the numbers.

My booking agent slotted all of the shows in, in between tours out of the province, after I got back from a couple of Yukon gigs, and before I left for Alberta.

I said I could only do four out of five school days in a row. I said I could only do a maximum of two shows a day. Okay, they said, but can you do three in a day if they are all in the same school? There will be no driving in between. We can feed you in the cafeteria, they said. Oh, and the gym seats 850. That's okay too, right?

I remember a kid on the first morning of the first show. He was tall and slender like a sapling, and I caught him pacing outside of the penumbra of gay-straight alliance kids who gathered around me for selfies after my show. He wanted to talk, I could tell, but he was too scared to be seen approaching the trans storyteller in front of his buddies. His friends meandered off to their next class one by one, but he remained, staring at his phone and watching me but never meeting my gaze directly. A buzzer wheezed from somewhere outside of the gymnasium and a distorted voice droned something I couldn't quite make out over the intercom, and the gym cleared out. I picked up my backpack and my water bottle and coffee mug, and asked the boy if he wouldn't mind helping me carry this microphone stand out to my car if that was okay. He leapt to my assistance, and followed me out of the side door of the gym and across the lawn to the parking lot. The grass was sparkling with frost still in the shadow of the school, and the sun was burning through the last of the fog lingering above the giant cedar trees in the greenbelt next to the football field.

He was silent until we got about 200 feet away from the school, and then he swallowed and the words fell out of him in one giant breath, only stopping for him to refill his lungs and then more words, like he had been waiting all of his, I don't know, maybe fourteen years for me to stand there in front of him and just listen.

He knew ever since he can remember, he told me, that he was into guys, but he had never told anyone. His brother would kick his ass, he said. Maybe his mom would be okay with it, and some days he even thinks she already knows he's gay, hard to say it's just little stuff she says sometimes but he's not ready to tell her anyway and he's supposed to get married to this girl in India, he's already met her and her family once last summer and he wanted to hate her but she's actually really pretty and nice and he liked her a lot which only made him feel worse because it's not fair since he already knows he can never be the husband she deserves to have because he's just not into girls and he's always known it and that is why he says he hates fags too whenever anyone brings stuff like this up and he didn't even want to like me but I was funny and he wasn't expecting someone to talk about bullying but somehow be interesting and funny even and if his dad ever found out he would kill him. And no, he doesn't mean his dad would be mad or homophobic, he actually means his dad would kill him for real, that is what his dad said when the Pride parade came on the news once he said if I ever see any of my sons marching with those perverts I will kill them dead quote unquote.

He talked and I mostly listened. How could I not? And what could I possibly say that wouldn't sound saccharine and empty? I bit my tongue on all the white sugar responses that rushed into my head and just heard him out.

Anything I can do to help you right now? I asked him finally, when he had stopped talking and looked around like he had just woken up, and then stared at the toes of his Nikes.

Nah, I don't think so. I just needed to tell you, I think? I dunno. You seemed like you would just get it, and not give me the number for a hotline to call or a rainbow pamphlet or something.

He looked at his phone. I'm way late for physics now.

I looked at my phone. I'm way late to get to my next gig now.

We looked at each other. He took a step towards me, and his shoulders jerked like he was moving in for a hug for a millisecond, but then he stuck out his hand and I shook it.

Yeah so, he said, and shrugged his narrow shoulders, and turned and loped back towards the front doors of the school.

I sat in the driver's seat of my car after for a minute, my head filling up and running over with half answers and reassuring but probably unrealistic things I never said to him.

I could tell you so many stories from that month of shows in Surrey. So many little stones still weighing down my pockets and gathered in the corners of all my everything.

Do I even tell you the story of the gender-neutral bathroom that someone, or, more probably, many someones had pissed all over? I had about 3 minutes after talking to some kids after my 9 a.m. show and when they started loading up the gym for the 10:30 show, and I ducked into the washroom right across the hall from the gym.

It took me only a few seconds to realize what was all over the floor, and the door handles, and all of the paper towel in the wastebasket. The toilet paper rolls in the dispenser were bloated and yellow with it too. Muddy and still-wet sneaker tracks on the countertop where they had stood to piss all over the mirror.

I turned on my Italian leather heel and walked back into the gym and found the principal. You might need to send a custodian into the gender-neutral bathroom, I told him.

He didn't blink. "What did they do in there this time?" he asked me, and didn't blink again when I described what exactly they had done in there this time.

That was the day I did three shows at the same school. No driving in between. But no bathroom, either, as it turned out. I didn't pee that day until a Starbucks just off the entrance ramp to the highway home, nearly four hours later. The dude behind the counter didn't even make me buy anything before he passed me the key. Tiny mercies.

There were also hundreds of shiny and beautiful stones, too. Supportive counsellors and pink-shirted principals and teachers trying, trying to fill in the gaps for their queer and trans students who had it hard at home, or who had already had to leave their homes.

But you're a teacher. I know you already know all of this.

I'm not writing this all down because I think you don't already know stories just like these ones. I'm writing to tell you I believe you. I'm writing you back to tell you I feel you standing right next to me on that stage, or in the face-off circle in the gym in front of all those rows of bleachers.

I'm writing to tell you that whenever you step into that classroom, whenever your heart pounds in that one-day crowded hallway again, and whatever they call you, I am right there beside you, too, and I see you. I'm grateful for your bravery. You will change that school faster and deeper and more fundamentally than any shiny-shoed storyteller ever can.

I'm so glad I got to meet you. I'm right here, too, on the other end of this letter that connects us now, ready to catch you at any moment.

Love your older (almost) brother,
Ivan

5.

DEAR FLORENCE

Dear Gran:

It's May 13 today, in the year 2020. Mom and Aunt Roberta went to Grey Mountain Cemetery this afternoon to put flowers out for you. Your eldest daughter called your youngest daughter, and then her sister called her older brother, and all four of your remaining children stood together around two cell phones and your gravestone and talked for a few minutes. Mom says the grass is still yellow but the snow is all gone for good, and the bright green buds are out on the willows and the poplar, and there were crocuses under that big pine tree.

It was eleven years ago today that we all squeezed ourselves into that tiny hospital room to bear witness and be with each other as you left this world. Eleven years. My mom's wristwatch stopped at 11:38 a.m. that morning, rendered motionless at the same moment you took your last breath. Someone noticed it hours later, and nobody was surprised. We are your sons and daughters and your grandchildren, and we all knew that you carried more than just a little magic inside of you. Part Roma, part Irish, part Jewish, raised in England. You have gifted us with this complicated lineage.

I have thought of you every day for the last eleven years, cross me heart, as you would say, I have. You live in me still in so many ways: you run in my veins, you appear in the lines around my mouth that echo the shape of your face when I turn mine just so. I felt you smile down on my sister and me so many times last summer when we picked berries together and made cranberry sauce from scratch without fighting, not even once. Carrie inherited your rocking chair, it sits now in the corner of her living room, right next to her little kitchen, and we could both feel you sitting in it and smiling when the lids on all of those jars popped, and I felt you again at the other end of that long highway days later, when I got home and stowed mine away in the cupboard.

I learned a while ago that Jewish people have a word for the anniversary of a loved one's death, they call it *"yahrzeit"* in Yiddish, originating from the German words *Jahr* and *Ziet*, meaning year and time. It is customary to light a candle at sundown inside of one's home or near the grave of the deceased. It is just now dark enough to light the candle on my desk for you.

It's been nine weeks now since the virus changed everything. I'm writing on this day to honour your memory and to thank you for everything you taught us, all those small and humble lessons you repeated so many times, they have become our prayers now. Go warsh yer hands. Save yer money. Finish yer suppa.

I remember when I was about ten years old you delivering a long lecture to all of us in the Qwanlin Mall parking lot after one of us complained about waiting in line at the SuperValu to pay for groceries. You told us about how in World War Two back in London, England you had to line up for everything: there was one lineup to buy flour, another to hope to buy a little meat, and another to get eggs, and how you had to save up enough sugar rations to make a cake if someone had a birthday, and how it taught you not to take things for granted.

I think about you now when I stand patiently six feet behind the person in front of me and six feet ahead of the next person in line outside of the grocery store.

You lived your nearly ninety years innately prepared for this moment in time, bleaching the kitchen counters and always eating the leftovers and clipping coupons and waiting for tomato soup to come on sale. I don't think you would have been surprised at all by the arrival of this virus at our doors, but even still, I've thought one hundred times how much I'm glad you didn't live to see these days unfolding, even though navigating through this new world makes me miss you multiple times every day.

I'm riding out the pandemic with my partner Sarah at her townhouse in London, Ontario right now. You never got to meet Sarah, and I'm sorry for that, too. We have a little poodle named Lucky that you would have deemed useless and lazy, but still let him sleep curled up close to your bony thigh on the couch, and fed him bits of cheese when no one was looking.

Sarah inherited this house from her grandmother, Kitty. Kitty smoked and drank until she fell and broke both of her legs walking down the third-floor stairs, and quit everything cold turkey without so much as a puff or a sip, ever again, for her last twenty years. We finally just yesterday ran out of the stash of dishwasher pellets she had socked away under the kitchen sink, we are on the very last box of medium-sized Ziploc bags she neatly stacked in the cupboard downstairs, and we still have two large rolls of her parchment paper in the third drawer in the kitchen, and Kitty died coming up on five years ago. We had to throw out some of her pantry full of canned goods because they expired before we could manage to eat that many red kidney beans and that much tomato paste. I think you and Kitty would have really liked each other, even though she didn't play bingo. Kitty didn't get out much. The little spruce tree she planted in her backyard in the mid-80s is thirty feet tall now, as is that once knee-high cedar hedge we planted around the same time in the front yard of your little house on Rosamond Street.

I can look out of the window next to the desk I am seated at while I write to you and see Victoria Hospital, where Kitty died in the summer of 2015. I sit with the ghost of one grandmother, and write a letter to the memory of mine.

One of the cruelest stories spun over and over by this virus is the one about old people dying alone in care facilities and hospitals, their families shut out and somewhere else, gathered around cell phones or iPads if they are lucky, to say goodbye, without a last touch, hands unheld and secrets carried out of this world unspoken. Only strangers there as witness. All faces masked and tears falling behind Plexiglas. I'm so glad I was there with everyone in the room in that moment for you, surrounded by your babies and their babies, and their babies too, all hands held and no tears spared. A sacred exit.

I have a pot roast in the slow cooker and its scent is calling me down the stairs to put the veggies on. The dog is sleeping on the bed next to me, a bed I made right after I got out of it this morning, the clean sheets tucked into tidy corners and the open ends of the pillowcases facing out, just like you taught us. Maybe tonight I will make pudding with the leftover rice from last night's dinner, with lots of cinnamon, so you will visit me in Kitty's kitchen. I will sweep the floor and put the kettle on, to conjure you up. The air will shift, and the birds outside will pause at the birdfeeder for a moment, and I will catch a whiff of Oil of Olay, and cigarette smoke caught in the pushed-up sleeves of an old grey cardigan with real bone buttons.

I can always tell when you have entered the room, even now, eleven years after you last left it.

I remain proud and grateful to be your first-born grandchild. I hope heaven is full of tailor-made Player's Light Regulars. I hope that your cough is gone and so are your bunions. I hope Uncle David is there too, but that he isn't bossing anyone around, or talking when your show is on.

Love always,
Ivan

6.

KIDS THESE DAYS

Hi Ivan,

I run into you every now and then at readings, so I think I know you, but don't really expect you to remember me since there isn't even a picture attached to this message. Anyway, reading your book *Rebent Sinner* (great title BTW), and crying at the appropriate places and probably not appropriate places too since my BFF of 50 years just passed and I am bereft lots of the time. But I have a good life and am really happy most of the time, so I will use her passing as commentary on what constitutes elders and where they/we have gone.

I was quite struck with your words about our LBGT++++ elders. With the departure from this world of my friend Sandy, who was a real live Native elder and the best friend anybody could ever have, I wondered too where our elders are. She was mine, and sometimes I was hers. She came out to me in 1971, when we were still illegal and still crazy. It was a huge risk, except that I was already contemplating my lesbianism at the ripe old age of 18. So she is gone. And I know that I have to become my own elder.

We are also losing Judy today—cancer. Sunshine Coast, cute as a button, fabulous politics—and as you opined, moved into pipelines, and NDP/Green and salmon. Queer politics gets you trashed. Been plenty trashed over the years. Frankly, given up. Playing music these days. Much better place to be. Except for the rampant sexism. But that's another story.

What I wanted to let you know really, is that we have become invisible. We're still here. And I would happily talk to the young ones. But they don't give a shit. I no longer get smiles or nods on the street when the cutest young couple walks by hand in hand. In choir, a young gal is wearing a Maui Pride shirt. Not a sign to me of acknowledgement. Not a fricking thing. And it's not like you have to guess. I look like a butch dyke. Maybe with a nicer haircut than I used to have. Is this left over from the patriarchy, where a woman over a certain age is no longer attractive so it's okay to ignore her? I don't know. But it drives me crazy.

Keep writing. I love that in Canada you, just as you are, can make a living telling your stories. I can laugh, I can cry, I can disagree with you. You are always interesting and you always make me think.

Still alive and kicking in Courtenay,
Syd Lapan

JULY 2, 2020

Dear Syd:

Let me begin with my condolences over the loss of your friend Sandy. I'm only 50, so I'm too young still to begin to be able to comprehend what the loss of a friendship you have had for 50 years must feel like. What secrets and memories and losses and triumphs and learning you must have witnessed and held for each other over those many decades. My tender heart to yours in your time of loss and grief.

I'm so sorry it has taken me this long to sit down and craft this letter to you. One of the biggest lessons that has revealed itself to me over the last four months since the pandemic arrived in our lives is how much human connection I was missing out on as a result of the relentless movement and touring and road that my life consisted of pre-pandemic. I was barely able to keep up with the constant stream of vital emails and booking and planning and quick correspondence: deep and thoughtful letters like yours would be starred or flagged, and filed away with every good intention of answering them when I had more than a minute to land, and rest, and catch up, and think. But those more than a minute moments were rare, and often I chose to go fishing or swimming or work on my cabin in the woods up north.

But here I am, at my girlfriend's place in London, Ontario, with our dog asleep against my left thigh, and my laptop actually resting in my lap, typing away while stretched out on top of the duvet, while the fan in the corner valiantly tries to move this humid air around the guest bedroom.

Like most of us during this lockdown, my life has slowed and grown much smaller. I had time to plunge my fingers into the cold black earth in the garden beds in our backyard back in early April, and to watch in reverence as tiny green tendrils surfaced and reached for the thin sun, and then grew inches overnight as that sunlight and its shadows stretched longer all through May. I have watched the peony stems swell into buds, and become round, and burst, and blossom, and then become brown and wilt and give themselves back to the ground. The spirea is thriving, and I am waiting for the lilies to make their first week of July debut, maybe tomorrow morning, or the next. I am learning the names and shapes of the birds here.

And I am answering all of those special letters.

Where to start? I looked up the word elder just now. The first definition is "a person of greater age than someone specified," or "a person of advanced age," or "a leader or senior figure in a tribe or other group."

I think the meaning of the word elder as we are both using it for the purposes of this discussion is to be found somewhere in between these definitions. Merriam-Webster is a little more nuanced maybe?

1) Of earlier birth or greater age 2) of or relating to a more advanced time of life or 3) superior in rank, office or validity

As I read and ponder all of these definitions, I am sure only of a few things. I may be older, but I'm not ready to be anyone's elder, just yet, and I for sure do not have enough elders of any definition in my life at the moment.

Both of my grandmothers are gone now, Florence in 2009 and Patricia in 2017. I think my seventy-year-old mother would cuff the back of my head if I called her an elder. I know she was simultaneously horrified and titillated a couple of years ago when a younger woman stood aside and let my mom and her partner Chuck cut to the front of the line at the annual Rendezvous Winter Festival pancake breakfast at the rec centre because they were "senior citizens now."

Queer elders, as we both know, are a different beast altogether. Maybe our queerness disappears a little as we age? Is that what happens? Maybe we slowly trade in our zippered black leather jackets and big motorcycle boots and blend in with the civilians once we have retired our uniforms? Maybe when we wear OUR Maui Pride shirts the kids just see an old woman who likes rainbows and comfortable shoes?

Sarah and I took the dog out walking along the Thames River a few months ago, when the goslings were still giant and clumsy melon-sized balls of yellow and grey fuzz. The buds were out on the trees but spring had yet to fully arrive still and I was grateful I had brought my warm jacket.

We passed by two older women sitting side by side on a bench that overlooked the water. One was knitting. Both were wearing purple shirts under their open jackets. One had a trace of a moustache and the other had a silver labrys pendant on a chain around her neck. I recognized them as family immediately, before either of them spoke to us. I almost always do. Sarah did not, and we talked a bit about this, and the two old lesbians in the car on the way home.

How do you know for sure they were lesbians? she asked me.

Are you kidding? I said. The purple shirts? The labrys necklace?

What's a labrys? She raised one manicured eyebrow at me.

Sarah is 40 and I am 50. She grew up in Sweden, and never really had to "come out" in the same way I had to back in the 80s. It was more commonplace in her circle of friends to be bi or queer in the much more liberal Sweden of her teens and twenties. The world had *The L Word* by then.

She mostly hangs out with other musicians of all sorts, and has spent very little time in the official queer community. She cannot clock an older lesbian quite as fast as I am able to, and frankly, older lesbians very rarely spot her.

I just re-read your letter. Imagined you and Sandy back in 1971, like you wrote, when you were 18 years old and still illegal and still crazy. The writer in me conjures up round-cornered Technicolor photographs of the two of you, in faded bell bottoms and plaid shirts, squinting into the camera, leaned up against a beat-up yellow VW Bug or a brown four-door Toyota Corolla. I was two years old, so that makes you . . . 67 years old now? Give or take. Still too young to lose your best friend. I'm going to take a guess and blame cancer. You say you have to become your own elder now, and just typing those words out, and contemplating what this means, brings me to tears.

You say that queer politics gets you trashed, and I find it hard to argue this point with you with much conviction, even though I so wish that this were not true. You say that you have given up on them, and I can't say I blame you too much. I have my moments of feeling like giving up myself, but my writing and my work keeps me tethered still, even when I want to escape. Hence the cabin I'm building up north, I guess.

My partner Sarah is a musician, too, so I often witness the sexism in the music industry that you mentioned. How when we walk into the theatre side by side to sound check for the show we wrote and tour together, the sound guy always defaults to talking to me, as the closest thing to a man that he can relate to. Sarah is actually the technical genius in the family, and the guitar and equipment wizard, and the composer, and the musical director, and the one who leads the six-piece band we tour with, but try telling Steve or Rick or Darryl the sound guy that he should be talking to the soft-spoken pretty one in the room, not the butch storyteller. They assume that I speak music bro more fluently than she can, even though music is Sarah's first language, and she can usually out-play, out-program, and out-delay pedal most of them on most days. So I often act as translator, by necessity. This sometimes makes me feel like a traitor, like I need to confess, or somehow cleanse myself of these masculine sins-by-association, but I am never sure where to go, or to whom to turn to in order to do this.

Whenever we walk into a venue and there are women technicians, I always make a mental note to make sure to come back, I can tell you that.

But back to your letter. I'm sorry you are invisible. At first I typed "I'm sorry that you feel invisible," but then I went back and deleted the word feel. If you say you are invisible, then I believe you that you are. So I will type it here again: I am so sorry that you are invisible.

I used to get called sir or be read as a man most of the time, but not so much the last couple of years, and hardly at all since the pandemic hit. I'm not sure exactly why this is. Is it a factor of the many weeks that have passed since my last trip to the barber shop? Is it these 51-year-old hips? The silver in my hair? Is it that I always without fail wear a mask when I go grocery shopping? Is it that I don't bother with a button-down shirt and tie, or my fancy show shoes while sheltering at home? I truly do not know.

What I can tell you is that being called a lady or ma'am still makes my teeth hurt and the inside corners of my mouth pinch like sucking on a really sour candy does. As strange as it sounds, being seen as a woman makes me feel like the opposite of invisible. It makes me feel intensely, mercilessly seen, or maybe mistaken for. I am not butch or trans or non-binary me. I am one of *those* women. I am the dyke next door. I am the not-pretty one of the two girls who moved into unit 705.

This is the little corner of the straight world I currently find myself in, anyway. I don't know how the cool young queer kids see me anymore, as it has been four months since I have seen any of them. I will report back once my online classes start up in September.

I miss the road, and doing shows, and faded and grimy green rooms and dusty black staircases threading through cluttered backstage mazes, and crowds of sweaty overdressed loud-talking queer people, more than I ever thought possible. Another thing the pandemic has taught me is how much I took all that road for granted, which, should all that road ever stretch out in front of my wheels in our currently unforeseeable future, I sincerely promise to never do again.

If I ever make it back to Vancouver Island, and if I ever see your face in person, I know in my butch heart that I will recognize you as my elder sister, and I swear to you that I will turn around and find the closest baby queer in the room and I will bring them over to where you are standing and I will say, Here, I want you to introduce you to Syd, she's a friend of mine, and I think you need to know her.

I hope I get to hear you play music one day, too.

Much love and solidarity,
Ivan

7.

SOLDIERS
WITHOUT
COUNTRY

Ivan. I have been following your travels via social media and I just can't believe the miles and countries you present in. It's all wonderful to think upon, but, yes, knowing the road from the inside out, I feel for you. I have often wondered if others feel that insane toppling, like falling from the Eiffel Tower when you first get back home from everywhere and feel yourself naked, undressed of commitments and timed events. I would so often feel like a billing envelope dropped in the alley, a grey rainy northwest alley. Everyone was so happy for me and I would confuse the hell out of them by weeping at their kitchen tables feeling like I had bullet wounds all through me. We didn't know back then about ptsd or the nature of trauma with all its myriad ways of presenting. I would feel so hollow, so empty, I was inconsolable. Over the years I learned to show a cool remove but even to think of that chaos now, brings tears brimming to my eyes. Ani DiFranco was betrayed by her audience and the passing of time and I have wept for her as well. So we truly are "soldiers without country" to quote an old Ferron song, capable of showing up in the trenches and disappearing on stage.

I have dreamt of doing a workshop with you at some point, somewhere. It's true what they say though in that there's a huge drop in physical endurance and things that once seemed easy peasy often stand just a little out of reach. But I think this spring I'm going to learn to stretch and grab. Here is my cell phone number. I suggest that we try to have a connection but I bet that you hear that from all the girls.

x, F

Dear Ferron:

It's Friday night on July 3, 2020. I'm at Sarah's place in London working in my little office here, catching up on letters and correspondence. I was searching through the last several years of Facebook messages for a note I got a few months ago from an older butch on Vancouver Island, and I came across this beautiful message from you.

I remember the morning I received it very clearly. I had just returned from an incredible but very gruelling tour of eleven cities in ten countries in Southeast Asia. I had been home for six days, and I was still jet-lagged, and physically suffering from an intestinal situation that I will spare you the details of, but suffice it to say I will never drink a fresh pineapple juice full of delicious yet suspicious crushed ice while petting rescued street dogs in a pen in Malaysia ever again. I only had to learn that lesson the one time.

I remember how my eyes filled up with tears and how I could suddenly hear my own heartbeat thrum past my eardrums as I read your words. I remember how my hands shook just a little as I reached for my cell phone and dialed your number, and how miraculous it was to hear you answer, hearing that deep and molasses-coloured and oh-so-familiar voice right there, live and in person, in my ear.

I think I tried to keep the fawning to a bare minimum, but I still do want you to know just how much a part of my life, my writing life, my road life, my inner and intimate and emotional creative life your music has been, for the last 32 years now, by my math.

The first girl I ever kissed was a jazz singer. Neither of us really knew any other queer people, not who were women, anyway, but her roommate's mom was a lesbian, and she had a partner and a cabin on Vancouver Island so the roommate called her mom the lesbian and set it all up and the jazz singer and I jump-started my Volkswagen van and went on a road trip to meet our people. Sheila and Jo. They fed us lentil stew and let us sleep in the octagon-shaped studio cabin and showed us lesbian books and lesbian poetry and three days later when we left Shelia gave me two cassette tapes: Joan Armatrading's self-titled album, and Ferron's *Shadows on a Dime*.

I listened to that tape until it wore thin and my tape player chewed it up and swallowed it, and so I bought it again. Then I bought it on CD, and I even found the LP in a thrift store on Commercial Drive and I bought that, too, even though it was 1995 by this time and I didn't own a record player. I eventually bought most of your other albums too, but *Shadows on a Dime* was my first and best love. I saw you live in Juneau, Alaska in 1992, and again at the WISE Hall in Vancouver. Your music, and your lyrics especially, are so much a part of my own writing practice now, your voice has accompanied the tap tap of my computer keyboard for all 12 of the books I have written. I learned to play many of your songs on guitar, and copied the lyrics into journals and learned them by heart. I fell in love all over again in a new way with Sarah a couple of summers ago when we learned to harmonize on the chorus of your song "Girl On A Road." I listened to *Shadows on A Dime* the first day home from every long stretch of touring, dog-tired and heartsore and the milk in the fridge all gone sour, crying on my couch from the grand toppling of it all while my laundry dried. Your music was a familiar place, an inherited quilt on the bed, a worn and favourite coin I kept in my pocket that my fingers knew all the edges and the weight of.

Those few months in early 2019 when we talked often on the phone were such a blessing to me, really, I don't know if I can shape the words right enough to explain it to you, but I will try.

I don't know very many butches who I connect with creatively. Most of my heroes that I resemble in any way are dead. I know butch carpenters and mechanics and chefs, and butch academics and filmmakers and parents and social workers, and I am truly grateful to have them in my life, but I didn't really have a personal connection to another living butch or trans or non-binary writer who was older and wiser than me until you sent me your cell phone number that December morning.

In early April of that same year, I experienced a bout of the worst online harassment I have ever lived through. I've had three serious, real-life stalkers, and I get my fair share of weird hate mail, but the spring of 2019 was next level. It was organized, and it was tech-savvy, and it was beyond mean. It was scary. A U.S.-based, ultra-right-wing Instagram account came after me online, and whoever was behind it had many minions. They created multiple accounts in my name and posted pictures of Hitler memes, and fathers feeding their trans babies bottles full of bleach and tagged my actual account in them, stuff like that. They tracked down the actual street address and suite number of the building I live in, and posted the information publicly, along with an invitation for their followers to go out and find me and, (and I quote) "visit this freak in person and tell it how you feel about it indoctrinating your children in public school to its vile trans lifestyle."

Upon the solid advice of an internet harassment professional, I went silent on all social media accounts, and tightened up and locked down all of my settings on all platforms for over a month, until the storm passed. I arranged to have a close friend monitor my messages, and forward me anything I needed to follow up on for work stuff. That is how I missed what happened on your Facebook page. At first, at least.

I got an email from a friend about it, along with some screenshots.

The sender knew about our friendship, and thought that I should know about the post you had written about trans women. It still makes me cry to think about it, these fifteen months later.

You are by no means the first friend of mine to reveal that you do not include trans women in your definition of what it means to be a woman. I have had to learn to allow many of my friendships to wither on this particular vine. I have mourned and argued and cajoled and begged friends of all stripes to come around and grow and listen and learn to truly see all of our sisters and siblings standing with us in this struggle for a better world, a better place to live alongside one another. Sometimes it has worked, slowly slowly. Often it has not.

We have not talked on the phone since that day. Your words, and the conversations and hateful comments that your original post allowed a space for, cracked my heart in half, and it is just now that I am able to put these thoughts in any sort of coherent order and send them to you.

I think we have spoken about how important both of my grand-mothers were to me. The respect and reverence that stills lives in my bones for both of them. I have always felt very blessed by their love and stories and guidance and their company around our collective kitchen tables. They were the sinew and the skeleton and the glue that held my giant family tethered together, and nothing has been the same at home or in my heart since they both left this realm. I was raised and kept closely connected by their blood, blood that bonded us all, a family that recog-nized both Florence and Patricia as our leaders, our rule makers, our ship's captains and our moral compasses. To say I was taught to respect my elders growing up is a vast and deep chasm of an understatement.

As a result, it is very difficult for me to write this letter to you. I'm unsure if you are even still reading it, but I have been drafting it in my head for a year and a half now, nearly, and it needs to be put to the page, not in spite of my great love and admiration for you and your music and mentorship, but because of it.

Please hear me when I say that I understand that many women who share your opinions with regards to trans women live with and sometimes die from foundational trauma, and deep, harmful and haunting memories of violence visited upon their bodies and their souls by men. Sometimes this trauma and this damage is inherited, and lives in the bone marrow, pacing and lurking and breathing all of the oxygen. I understand this, I really do.

Also please hear me that trans women, and trans men, too, and non-binary people like myself, have to conjure and create ourselves out of that very same broken and bleeding bone marrow, and have to fight to exist in the very same patriarchal system that would disappear all of us if we let it, without seeing any difference at all between you, and me, and trans people of every variety. I truly believe that we are all equally expendable to those powerful structures we exist in, and around, and outside of. We are all often standing or sitting or kneeling outside of the very same gates of power, asking for many of the same rights over our own battered bodies, and demanding the same or similar dignities from the same uncaring or oblivious ears.

I know from your lyrics that you are a warrior, a soldier without a country, a deep thinker, and a wounded lover.

I know from our many talks last year that you are also funny, and eccentric, and heartsick, and sometimes profoundly lonely.

I want you to know how much I miss our friendship, and our mutual support, and our newly-hatched creative connection. I'm not sure if there is any conversation we can have that you haven't already had with hundreds of others wiser and more eloquent than I am that could ever convince you to open your heart and make room at your hearth for trans people, especially trans women, who are some of the bravest and most misunderstood women I know.

I'm writing to tell you that I miss you. I am writing to tell you that I am still here, and I love you, and I am willing to have many and all of the hard conversations with you if it might mean that I could have you back in my life again in some meaningful way. I write this letter to you knowing that we might never agree about this topic, even though I see so much of my own truth in the lines around your eyes, and in your poetry, and in the stories of your life, and I know in my heart that trans women are my sisters, so they must be your sisters too, if you allow yourself to listen and hear where their stories run alongside both of ours, not over, or across, or against them.

You might be shaking your head right now at me, if you are still reading, but you still have my number, and I promise to bring all of my compassion, and my best ears, and all of my love and respect for you to that kitchen table.

I'm writing you this letter so I can play your records again, and hear your voice without thinking about how I need to write you this letter.

I'm writing you this letter because I can no longer bear the thought that the last thing that rang out in the space between us was my silence.

with much love and hope,
Ivan

NOVEMBER 9, 2020

Dearest Ferron:

I'm writing you again, about 48 hours after Joe Biden was declared to be the president-elect of the United States. I believe you're still in Arizona, am I right about that? I just checked the red and blue map on CNN and the electoral college vote has not yet been declared there, coming up on a week after election day, and some would say that means it doesn't matter now what happens in Arizona, Biden has won, and that is all that is important.

I wonder, though, how this feels for you, walking your little dog to and from your local park, or leaning over to pick the right bunch of celery at the grocery store, or lined up with your neighbours outside of the bank—do you glance at the people you live next to and ask yourself inside who they voted for? Can you tell just by looking at them most times? Do you wonder if the man standing behind you in the lineup at the supermarket voted against your right to control your own body, did he vote to keep locking up children in border camps? Does his spiritual advisor also speak in tongues?

What about the woman in the park with the geriatric Pomeranian, who gave you a jar of peaches she canned herself last fall, and who checked Trump on her ballot but when asked says she doesn't even tell her husband who she voted for? To me, she's scarier than any red-hat-wearing camouflage-vested blowhard will ever be.

I'm glad you have your sweetheart with you, and that you have a little garden, but I have to be honest and tell you that I worry about you still. I worry about all of my friends in the U.S. a tiny bit less this morning than I did last week, but still. My concern for the safety and human rights of all of my American friends has been around for all of my adult life now, and I don't expect any election will ever change that, not in my lifetime, anyway.

I want to sincerely thank you for the phone calls and conversations we have had over the last few months. I really appreciate you taking the time to talk it all through with me. Thank you for forgiving me my long silence. I needed the time to think, to put each of my words in the proper and peaceful order, to craft my measured response to you, my very dear friend.

I understand that your initial reaction and post on social media was one born and carried in the marrow of your own trauma response, and your own reflex-driven protective arm of solidarity with another woman who you saw as being threatened by someone that you did not recognize as another woman.

Sometimes when offering up yet another argument feels like wheelbarrowing already-dry concrete up a mountain, I find a story is easier to lift up. So I will tell you one of my stories.

Three summers ago, on a beautiful July day, I left my apartment to walk one and a half blocks up Hastings Street to go to the market for groceries. I had just landed back home from a long stretch of road, again, very late the previous night, and I know I don't need to tell you about that exhausted and elated but heart-worn feeling I held in my chest as I squinted into the sun and set out to fetch some food to fill my empty fridge and belly with. I didn't even have any coffee beans left, so I ventured outside, my skin confused by the change from air-conditioned lobby to sweaty streetside.

I was about ten paces from my front door when it happened. Something big and unseen struck me hard from behind and pushed my body forward and down, my knees, then my elbows striking sidewalk, and the side of my head ringing off of the thick plate-glass window of the travel agency that makes its home in one of the commercial units on the ground floor of my building.

I heard her voice then, the woman on the bike that had knocked me over, and her face spun and then swam into focus above me. "Are you a fucking dude or a chick? Hard to fucking tell." One corner of her thin mouth was peeled up in a question mark, her eyes narrow and mean. Then she pedalled away.

A tornado of rage left a skid mark of circles in my head. I tried to breathe and realized I couldn't, not yet, that all of my air was still outside of me, waiting for me to be able to inhale again. I was on my hands and knees on the concrete next to my neighbour's doormat. I felt like jamming my fist into the spokes of that woman's bike and toppling her off of it, but by the time I could take a full breath and stand up again, she was long gone. A bus stopped on the opposite side of the street, belched out some of its passengers, and then puffed and hissed off. Traffic continued to hum. My ears were ringing. Little black stars glinted behind my eyelids when I blinked. A man walking a pit bull made a wide comma around me, staring at me but saying nothing.

I guess I could have chased the woman on the bike, maybe even caught up to her while she waited for the light to change up the block, if she was the wait for the light to change type. But what then? I look like a man, most days to most people, and she was a wiry little white woman with dirty long blonde hair. To most eyes I would be a decently dressed dude, yelling at a visibly poor woman on a beat-up ten-speed on a Hastings Street corner in East Vancouver.

So I picked the gravel out of the heels of my palms and inspected the torn-out knee of my good show jeans that I had just put on, pressed a bloodied flap of my skin sort of back into place, and went to buy myself an already-made coffee at my friend's shop up the block. I was hoping Marc would be there, so I could get some sympathy, or a joke, or at least a free Americano, but one of his employees told me he was out and wasn't expected back until late afternoon.

So I sucked it up. Tried to shake it off. My head still hurt. My teeth didn't feel quite like they fit together right yet. I found blood on my elbow, too, and my shirttail.

This is not the first story like this I have lived through, and still carry around with me. The last time I got punched in the face by a woman was long enough ago that it was because I wouldn't get off of the pay phone she needed to use fast enough, and I did the same thing back then, too. I sucked it up, fists curled but held firmly at my sides. Rage swallowed silently. A deep-seated survival tactic known to almost every trans person I have spoken to about such things. We are not often afforded any opportunity to fight back, not with our angry words, and certainly never with our fists or our deeds. Our responses must always be measured, and spoken softly, and without carrying any whiff of threat, any form of confrontation. Anything else will too easily be weaponized against us. See, how the masculine one is always so aggressive? See, I told you they're all just men wearing dresses. See, I told you.

Even when our rights are under direct attack. Even when our children, or children like us, are being denied compassionate care. Even as images of our deaths are being shared online and labelled as allyship, as solidarity. We must take a deep breath, unclench our jaws and knuckles, and be patient, and peaceful, and reconciliatory, or risk being labelled as the violent ones.

Have you read the recent interview with gender theorist Judith Butler in the *New Statesman*? I can send you the link if you are interested in reading the full piece. In my reading of the article, Butler is being interviewed by a woman who is barely interested in concealing her bias, hardly pausing to sweep sand over her TERF tracks at all. The interviewer is questioning Butler about definitions of "the category of woman" and who it is exactly that feminism purports to be fighting for.

Throughout the lengthy grilling, Butler displays their signature level and scalpel-sharp theory. Unshakable and not to be trifled with. There are no less than thirty quotes from Butler in this article that I hope to one day commit to memory, but my favourite exchange is this:

> **AF** (Alona Ferber, the interviewer): "How much is toxicity on this issue a function of culture wars playing out online?"

> **JB:** "I think we are living in anti-intellectual times, and that this is evident across the political spectrum. The quickness of social media allows for forms of vitriol that do not exactly support thoughtful debate. We need to cherish the longer forms."

We need to cherish the longer forms. I have repeated that sentence in my head a thousand time since I first read it. And then there is the next question:

> **AF:** "Threats of violence and abuse would seem to take these 'anti-intellectual times' to an extreme. What do you have to say about violent or abusive language used online against people like JK Rowling?"

> **JB:** "I am against online abuse of all kinds. I confess to being perplexed by the fact that you point out the abuse levelled against JK Rowling, but you do not cite the abuse against trans people and

their allies that happens online and in person. I disagree with JK Rowling's view on trans people, but I do not think she should suffer harassment and threats. Let us also remember, though, the threats against trans people in places like Brazil, the harassment of trans people in the streets and on the job in places like Poland and Romania—or indeed right here in the US. So if we are going to object to harassment and threats, as we surely should, we should also make sure we have a large picture of where that is happening, who is most profoundly affected, and whether it is tolerated by those who should be opposing it. It won't do to say that threats against some people are tolerable but against others are intolerable."

I want you to know, Ferron, how much I truly cherish the opportunity to have this long conversation with you. I appreciate your patient ear, and that you are taking the time to consider these issues.

Another story: when Sarah and I were first really falling in love with each other, I put on your record *Shadows on a Dime* and when the needle got to that song "Proud Crowd" I started to sing along, like I always do.

And that is when I heard Sarah singing along on her grandmother's old plaid pullout couch beside me, word for word for word.

Hey, I said, you are the only other person I know who knows all of the lyrics to this song.

Her eyes were shining with tears and she smiled at me. You are the only other person I know who knows all the lyrics to this song, she confessed.

To this day, I swear on all things holy, whenever we have a fight we quote your lyrics to each other, until forgiveness is found, and conceded:

I can't call you from this place
To hear you say that I'm not your kind

It's a thin road before us, we're the wake left behind
It's sad and I fail to see what it had to do with you and me
But I guess that's like wondering what's a point to a line

There must be something I wanted more than wanting your love
'Cause you stood in my doorway and I stood in my glove
Most afraid to follow, a kingdom my stride
It's so telling what won't live with hunger and pride

I thought of you often but I never could tell you
The "you" that I cherished, something hurt me so bad
A few had come close, I couldn't take them in either
I guess the distance between us was my love never had

And though we live separate I keep two rooms open
One has you in it, the other does not
And I move in the middle, unsure and protected
And I trip on my rope, vaguely sensing I'm caught

True story. Your lyrics are now our peace offering to each other.

So. Thank you for reading this, Ferron. Thank you for loving me enough to pick up that phone. Thank you for not standing in your glove.

I know that the heart that crafted those lyrics is a loving and changeable one.

It's a heart that I cherish, and that I will not ever give up on.

I also promise to always come to the table ready to listen.

With love and respect,
Ivan

8.

EVERYTHING HAS CHANGED

Dear Ivan,

Thank you for listening to your grandmother and sharing your gifts with the world. I'm the guy who tried to talk to you at the end of your morning Teachers Convention session but found words failed me. Thanks for the hug. A couple months ago you were in Calgary for a reading at the library. Before your show my son had you sign his book and you offered him a hug too. He is a very big fan of you and your writing.

Here's my story. I'm the father of a wonderful, courageous, cynical, hilarious transgender son. I'm also a high school English teacher. I was delighted that my kid wanted to come to my school. I didn't realize that my kid was looking for a fresh start. In the fall of grade ten, my daughter came out to me as gay. Cool. That would have been tough when I was in high school, but we have a GSA at our school, my brother is gay, this will likely mean some bumps in my kiddo's road but we offered our full support. All was well. Rainbows were everywhere. In the fall of grade ten, my daughter told me she had come out of the wrong closet. "I'm transgender, Dad." My immediate reaction (internal) was of confusion and disbelief. We agreed you were gay. That was part of my landscape. That made sense . . . Externally, I was verbally supportive. Several internet searches later, I was led astray. What I came across was the "sudden onset dysphoria" camp. I am very sorry that I landed there. My wife and I decided to wait and see. Yes, we were in denial or avoidance mode or both. But my son (who I was still calling my daughter) was insistent. One day I was down the hall while my kiddo was doing their homework at the dining room table. "Nothing's changed," they hollered from down the hall. They hollered this phrase three times before I came down the hallway to investigate. Gifted parent that I am, I recognized that my kiddo wanted to talk to me. So I agreed that we would go and find support. We made two appointments for the second week of February 2019. They were both on the same day. The first appointment saw us go to the mental health people at our local medical clinic. The therapist we met asked a lot of questions that my kid answered vaguely. I think they were convinced that this was not where they'd get help. It was me who first used the word transgender in that meeting. I said that I didn't understand what was going on and I said that I'd been disgusted with my high school-aged body, my sister had always hated her body . . . isn't this what's going on? The therapist gave my kiddo a look and then said to me in a tone that sounded rather weary, "Gender dysphoria is a bit different than that. You understand that, don't you?" I don't remember much of the rest of the meeting, but we made a follow-up appointment for a one-on-one session for our troubled teen. Our next appointment was at a place called Skipping Stone. We drove across town and found our way to their office. The moment my kiddo walked into their space, their body language changed. The first person we met was Louise, one of the co-founders of the organization. She looked at our perfect child and said, "What is your chosen name? What are your pronouns?" Atticus introduced himself and his physical self transformed before our eyes. His body language relaxed and he smiled a huge smile. And I got it. This is the new reality. We talked a lot with this amazing woman in the Skipping Stone offices. Atticus was hooked up with a counsellor, my wife and I were invited to a monthly parent meeting, my mind was reeling but I was on board. We'd set out looking for help for our kid, but it was the parents who needed to be educated. The next little while was a whirlwind for us. I noticed Atticus reading a book his cousin Sarah had given him: *Tomboy Survival Guide*. His nose was always in that orange book. For the rest of grade eleven, Atticus was himself at home. We used male pronouns and we used his name. Except for when we screwed up— and we screwed up a lot. Atticus has a younger brother and a younger sister. They got it as soon as he told them. And he told them before he told us. So they were relieved that they could call Atticus by his name in front of us. At the end of grade eleven I notified Atticus's teachers and other key adults in the school that he would be socially transitioning at school. We shared the news with family and close friends. In the space of a few months I had become a crusader for gender-neutral washrooms and LGBTQ rights—particularly trans rights. It's been a year, almost to the day, since we started calling Atticus by his correct name and refer- ring to him by his correct pronouns. We had a father-and-son date back in the fall when we went to your reading at the Calgary Public Library. Atticus's teachers and classmates have been supportive, for the most part. My kid is a champ in the classroom: eighties are normal fare for him. But he is hurting so much and we continue to worry about his mental health and his safety. He's been on testosterone for six months. His voice has dropped. I think his face has changed, especially around the jawline. He's happy to be on T, but he is still very repulsed by his body. He hates to shower. He's binding some days and taping others. He has terrible sores from the tape but when he tapes he can breathe. He's on a waiting list for top surgery and we don't know how long the wait will be in the current political climate. Our doctor, a specialist in trans- gender care, is cautiously optimistic. I am just hoping that Atticus can face the future with some semblance of hope. Your writing inspires him. Thank you for providing Atticus and so many other people with a per- spective that reflects their experiences.

So as I sat in your presence today, so grateful for you sharing your stories, my kiddo was in my heart. And every struggle that you mentioned had me thinking of Atticus and the road he is on. I agree with you that transgender kids are tough and resilient. I don't know anyone braver than my boy. He's a wonder. He's opened my eyes and my heart to the transgender journey. This has helped me enormously as a teacher and as a human being.

Thank you for cracking my heart wide open, Ivan.

Sincerely,
Lee

Dear Lee:

I first read this letter from you on Friday, February 14, about an hour or so after you sent it to me. I remember the moment very well, because I was exhausted from the conference gig I had done the day before, the evening flight to Calgary on Thursday night, and the early morning and the two events at the teacher's conference I had done that day. The first, the 9 a.m. workshop, was the one you were in. I can still remember your face, and your tears, and the hug you gave me afterwards.

I was about to fly home for a couple of days off and my road defenses were in the early steps of dismantling themselves. I had just eaten a salad with avocado and grilled chicken on it at the Chili's in the domestic departures wing. I have come to know Ernest, the very gay waiter there, over the last few years, and we had chatted about his mother's poor health, and his sore feet, and my lower back troubles.

My back was killing me that week. That month. That winter. I was having difficulty leaning over to retrieve my charging cable out of my backpack, and I had just taken the last of the pink pills my doctor had prescribed to me for the pain. I had been out of town so much in the previous weeks I hadn't had time to refill the prescription. Bulging disc. Sciatic pain down my right leg that sometimes drops me right to my knees when it seizes my spine and flares down my right thigh towards my toes. I blame all of those airplane rides. All those hotel beds. All those suitcases in the overhead compartments. I blame two and a half decades of road.

I knelt to plug my phone into the flickering receptacle under my seat in the crowded departure gate, lowered myself gingerly into my curved plastic seat, and read through my email. I read this letter from you. The tears were rolling before I even got to the end. I know it's been said too many times, and by too many people, but for real, and sincerely, it is letters like yours that help me get through days like that.

I have lost count of how many departure lounges I have sat in and let the tears roll down my face. My friend Bear calls this crying like a storyteller. My girlfriend calls it road malaise. I call it Friday night in the departure lounge again.

I heard someone say excuse me, and then they repeated those two words, excuse me, excuse me two more times, until I looked up. Blue hair, shaved on one side. Snow boots over torn jeans. A ukulele propped against the empty seat beside them. A phone dangling a white cable and charger in one hand. "Are you the writer? Are you Ivan Coyote? You came to my school in Lethbridge a couple of years ago. I bought your book *Tomboy Survival Guide*. Can you plug my phone in for me?"

The truth was I didn't think I actually could bend over again and plug their phone in, not without my back fully going into a spasm. I apologized and said that my back was really hurting me, and shuffled my butt over to make room for them to get to the plug under my seat.

"Hey, are you okay?" They squinted at me once they noticed the tears in my eyes.

I pretended I was crying because of my very sore back, not over a letter from the father of a trans son. I put my phone down, and proceeded to make small talk with the kinesiology student with the English minor until my plane began to board.

I wrote you back the following Sunday and thanked you for your email, and promised I would answer you properly when I had a little time off.

It's July now and I'm in Ontario, where it is 40 degrees Celsius outside if you count the humidity, which I have learned to do, and I haven't done a face-to-face show, or taken an airplane ride, in months. My back pain has all but disappeared, and (and I'm not even convinced this is physically possible) my hair has substantially less grey in it than it did when I last saw you at the convention centre in Calgary back in February.

I've wondered a thousand times since the pandemic first hit and the schools all closed their doors and went online, about all the queer and trans kids (well, I've worried about all of the kids, truthfully, but I admit, I do save a helping of especially poignant and painful concern for the queer and trans kids) who are now at home all summer, and what it has been like for them without school hallways, and school buses and school gymnasiums and classrooms, and maybe still no school this September. I imagine some of them are relieved, and free to some degree now of the scrutiny and cruelty of their classmates and peers. I also know that for some kids, school is the safest place that they know. I remember vividly, early in my school gig career, learning that even my most terrifying and traumatizing memories of high school shrink and fade to almost nothing compared to what some kids face down every day in unsafe homes, hunkered down under hostile roofs, seeking shelter deep within dangerous territory. Some of us escaped from school, and some of us escape into it, and I try never to forget that.

But I don't need to tell you this, because you are an English teacher, and a father, and I am neither of those things.

I came out as queer to my mom when I was 18, and slowly, mostly from her reading my books, as trans when I was in my early forties. I let my words on pages say all the things I was too afraid to tell her in person. In a way, this means I was more honest with audiences full of strangers than I was with my own mother. I told them first, and she found out by reading published public truths that spoke to who I was. I'm not sure if I forgive myself for this, so I don't dare ask her to.

If I could change one thing about our relationship, I would wind the clock back three decades or so and sit us both down for a really honest talk. I would be 18 or 19, and she would be 38 or 39. I would make myself tell her who I really was, and I would make her tell me truthfully what she felt about it all. I would make us tell each other all about what we were most afraid of.

I was a small-town kid who didn't even really know any other queer people. I don't think that I had even whispered the word trans yet into the mirror. I knew nothing of my history. I had no role models, or examples, or proof of a future for myself. My mom was a same-small-town Catholic girl with an older brother who was both a bully and a priest, born from a devout mother who was very good at keeping everyone's secrets, especially her own. My mom was not only very practiced and adept with keeping up with the Joneses, she had grown up right next to them, and their dad drank with her dad, and she had dated the oldest son back in high school.

Everything about my hometown always happens right across the street from everything, and everyone, else.

I wish so much I wasn't still afraid of who I was when I first told her about myself, and I wish she had told me that she was way more afraid of what the world was going to do to her queer kid than she was that her kid was a queer. Mistaking that fear for her shame cost us years and years of wasted tears.

I guess what I'm saying is, is that you and Atticus have about a thirty-year head start on me and my mom, and I love her almost more than any other human, ever.

Have you seen the documentary *Disclosure* on Netflix yet? I cannot recommend that you watch it enough. I want you to watch it, and then call me after. I want it to heal you like it healed me. It is about the mostly negative portrayal of trans people, mostly trans women, in media. It takes apart the kinds of stories that are told about us in movies and television, over and over, and how those stories hurt us, by shaping the stories that cisgender people hold in their heads when they see us, or don't see us, what they conjure up when they imagine us, and who they imagine us to be.

There is a part of the documentary where they interview the actor Jen Richards, I'm going to watch it again so I can get the quotes from her just right. She is talking about hearing a father speak about his trans son.

Jen Richards: " . . . and there was a scene where there were parents talking about their kids."

Unnamed father (from documentary footage): "If you have a transgender kid, you are living with a unicorn, an amazing human being. To be next to someone so brave, so cool, so close to themselves. The reality is that Avery has been on point from age two, apparently. Know what I mean? So the reality is it's such an honor."

Jen: "I was watching this father, and it just . . . it hurt, because I had to be okay with my mom saying, 'I will never call you Jen because Jen murdered my son.' I had to—I had to be okay with that, in order to survive myself, you know? In order to deal with not being able to see my grandma before she died, because I could only come home if I dressed as a boy. You know? I had to deal with the fact that one of my best friends, who, like, I stood up at his wedding, won't let me meet his children. I have to deal with those things, like, I have to live with those things. And I have to make that okay. I have to understand their position, and be okay with it. And when I saw that father go so much further than I thought was even possible, it hurt, I couldn't bear it because then, all of a sudden, all those people who couldn't accept me . . . when I knew it was possible to go *beyond* acceptance? Why couldn't my mom have been like him? That's the question I never asked until that moment. Why couldn't my mom have been like him? Why couldn't my friends have been like him, and seen the value in my experience? But the person who is most responsible for failing to have that kind of vision is me. I have never seen myself the way that father saw his own child. I'd never seen myself that way. I'd never looked at myself with the kind of love and respect and awe that that father had for his own child. No one's looked at me that way. How could I look at me that way? I had to see it. And now that I have, I want that." (She then inhales deeply, exhales, and takes a sip of something from a sky-blue coffee mug).

It is this less-than-two-minute clip from this documentary that is still rattling around in my heart, a month later, bruising me from the inside.

I thought of you, Lee, when Jen was talking. I was already writing you back in my head, so how could I not conjure you and Atticus up?

I don't speak to my dad about who I really am very much. He loves my partner Sarah, and respects her, and loves her music, and he is kinder to her than he is to me, and that is mostly enough for me. He gets my name right almost half of the time around me, but calls me by my deadname to his friends still, I suspect. I know he loves me, but these facets of who I am embarrass him. All of this about me seems to be . . . inconvenient for him. I manage to be patient when correcting him about my name, which I changed 27 years ago now. I don't even try to get him to comprehend my choice of pronoun. He is 72 years old, and an alcoholic struggling increasingly with dementia. I pick my battles, and this is one I know there is no winner for, and I do not have the heart to pick up my arms to fight him. If I could bottle the hurt all of this has caused me, and get him to take even a sip of it, I know he would try harder, but to be honest, it would be a drip in a river of guilt he feels about his failings as a parent, and as a man, and I am too merciful to do that to him at this point. He might not remember it all the next day anyway, and that might just crush me.

Why am I telling you all of this? Is this too much information? Did you really want to know any of this about me when you sat down in front of your computer in February? Is July too late to talk about any of it?

I'm crying now as I type. I have worked very hard for years to not feel ashamed of my tears, to allow myself to fully feel things, to describe them, to share them. To craft them into the shape of a story. This is what I know about stories: they can tear me up on their way out of me, but they rarely leave a scar. I am healed in a way, just by the telling.

Please sit down with Atticus and read him the letter you wrote to me, and read him my letter back to you. I want him to see your love and care for him in your words, shining from these pages like they do. I want him to see his future glinting. I want him to know that he will grow up and one day be someone's hero, someone's roadmap, and role model. Maybe even someone's father.

I think you are the kind of father who, if he could, would put yourself in between any harm or hurt the world might aim at your children, but you can't do that. There will never be enough of you to do that. This world is full of far too many people who actively work to make life difficult for trans people, and there are even those who would disappear us if they could. But there will never be enough of them to do that. They can never will us, or deny us, or legislate us, out of existence.

We are here, as we always have been.

Every new generation is born to parents who, at some point, will not understand their children. I've never curled up under the covers and cried because my father didn't understand me, but I still weep even as I write to you today, because he didn't listen, and he doesn't ask, and he won't try. You did, and you do, and you are.

I hope this letter finds you and Atticus, and the rest of your family well, and thriving. Please do let me know how school is this fall, for both of you. Please give Atticus a hug from me, until the world turns enough that I am able to hug him again myself.

With much love and admiration,
Ivan

9.

ALL OF YOU

Hi Ivan,

I attended your storytelling session at the research and statistics conference today in Terrace. After hearing from Robert Pictou and then you, I was feeling quite vulnerable, on the cusp of crying if I tried to express to you then all the things I wanted to say. Which, now seems ironic and shows me just how much work I still have to do on myself, when you had mentioned the way in which emotion is considered a feminine thing, and therefore a weak thing and while my peers nodded I could only worry that in reality they may not be so understanding.

I'm a cisgender female, mostly closeted bisexual, and was raised in a conservative Christian home and school. So when I heard an LDS colleague strike up a conversation about religion, I eavesdropped. I loved your response, never dismissing faith but dismissing the way it has been perverted, from love and inclusion to hate and exclusion. From a recognition of the beauty of the human spirit and body in all forms reflecting the ungendered god, to this small limited acceptance of some forms. As a younger adult I attended a Christian college, and came home after one semester declaring I wanted to switch programs and become a pastor. My father and I fought, which ended when I told him God did not create me this way, but his sperm did. And while that is flawed, I realize now that truly my upbringing has stripped me of the confidence to do the things that interest me. Or to not even consider some things as an option for myself. His words and the church's rules truly did set me upon a specific path. As a Research Analyst at my institution this distrust in my own abilities as a queer woman meant I didn't even apply for the job in the first place. Until the male manager recruited me. For the first two years I didn't believe I had the math or logic skills, as that is a man's brain, and the school I had grown up in left me with a grade 8 level math and I never attempted a math course in college. Two years before I trusted I could count, three before I felt like I understood just what I was counting—I'm coming up on my fourth anniversary in the job and I've finally taken a first-year university level stats course. Which I aced. I'm also enrolled in a database administration program, a male-dominated profession, and finding success—but more than that, finding that I've been doing that work all along but without those labels that have intimidated me in the past. That were not for me. And as you talked about data and representation, I realized just how seeing myself in those classrooms, jobs, or program catalogues as a young person might have changed my life, my self-confidence and self-awareness of my abilities. How much more so for the students I report on now—for the successes we celebrate and highlight in our reporting to truly reflect the diversity of our student body so these wonderful perspectives and brains aren't thrust into a small narrow corridor leading to only one or two possible outcomes or careers. That we start programming ourselves from such an early age to decide where we can find success, where we see those like us succeeding. And how I can heal myself by intentionally providing this for someone else, that this can be a role in which I do impact someone's life, even as I sit in a tiny office behind a computer screen all day.

Hearing someone acknowledge something so simple as you have been discouraged from discovering your full potential, and that wasn't right. In a conference where I feel uneducated compared to my peers, unable to contribute to discussions because I don't trust my own judgement, to have someone send the message that you are capable of more than what everyone else has been telling you, without actually then following it up with "and this is what you're capable of . . ." really just sewed up this little patch of my teenage ragged heart that has just barely hung in there through the years. Thank you. I wanted to say thank you, in person, but I don't think I could have gotten any other words out. Your work is so much bigger than youth, but so important to them specifically, and so I wanted to say thank you for providing those words, that widening of options beyond gender, and empathy for, and non-dismissal of faith, and the immediate acceptance that being queer, feminist and faithful is not an oxymoron—all those messages you give to the youth you encounter, thank you. From teenage me, to adult me. To those at the messy cross-sections of things a society and family says can't exist, the acknowledgement without asking for an explanation is freeing. Is validating that I do exist the way I think I do, and I'm really not alone. I cannot express fully just how healing and hopeful that makes me.

This a messy and discombobulated email, in which my intention was just to tell you thanks. And to let you know that as a group we've been opening up to each other, and have been talking about your stories all evening. This new level of vulnerability really will change our relationships to our colleagues, to our work—it has inspired us to reconsider the importance of our jobs—as public employees who truly are there to serve the students, even as we report to deans or VPs. And how we might influence change just by recognizing what we don't report or how we group individuals together or make distinctions where they are unnecessary and adjusting as appropriate.

I am so grateful that our paths crossed just briefly enough to hear a few words I never knew I needed, that they were from a stranger who made my experience seem a little less strange was an added blessing.

Prayers to you on your journey home, for your family in this time of loss, may you find the support you provide to strangers in the company of your family and friends through this time.

Melinda

Dear Melinda:

Thank you for your beautiful letter. Before I begin to do it any justice, please let me start with apologizing to you that it took me three years, one month, and, so far, ten days to answer you. If it makes any difference, your email has sat in a starred folder in my inbox all of this time, because the moment I first read it, I knew it was one of those letters, the ones that I really had to sit down and search inside of me to respond to properly.

I remember the day we met very well. I remember you. You were sitting at one of the large round tables, on my left, near the back of that beautiful longhouse at the university in Terrace, close to the fold-out tables at the back that held the coffee urns and the croissants and the muffins. It was June 9, 2017, like you wrote, which means my grandmother Patricia had been dead for eleven days. I was in Australia when I got the 2 a.m. call that she had died, and I had to do one last puffy-eyed and numb-hearted show that night in Byron Bay, before I flew back to Vancouver, via Sydney, then Auckland, then Los Angeles, and then finally up to Whitehorse to be with my family. I remember being so tired and jet-lagged the night before that conference in Terrace that I hallucinated a large house cat streaking across the carpet in my hotel room. It turned out to just be the air conditioner making the draperies dance in front of the flickering glow from the television. I think that is when I got up and took a Nyquil to help me get to sleep. Not an excuse, just a description of where my head was at those few weeks after my grandmother passed. My touring schedule has historically very little mercy when it comes to family emergencies, and the grieving process. I usually save up all of my mourning and breakdowns and breakups for the months of December and January, when the road slows down enough to allow me time for them.

But here we are in July, hoping that stage three re-openings of gyms and restaurants and swimming pools province by province won't usher in a surge and a second wave of the virus, and I am finally writing you back.

I do recall, while I was preparing my storytelling sessions for that day, wondering just why I had been invited to speak to a room full of statisticians and mathematicians, and why they cared to listen to a transgender writer tell stories anyways, but then I met you all, and told some stories, and you listened, and you laughed and cried, and then I listened to your questions, and we talked, and the sense of it all started to take shape in my head.

I remember that question from the evangelical Christian woman. I have had to learn, over the years, to tactfully field questions aimed at me from evangelicals of all stripes. And it is true, what I said to her that day. I don't remember my exact words, but I know in my heart what I believe, and I know what it was that I had been asked to come there and do, and I have grown to consider these moments as divine opportunities for me to do what I think of as something close to sacred work.

When a person who has been taught, like I knew immediately that she had been taught, to hate and revile me stands up to ask me a question, I must reach across that room and find my way past her fear and dogma and doctrine and into the good part of her heart. But to locate that part of her heart I must make myself truly believe that it exists, even if her body language or words are screaming otherwise, or I might miss it in the dark and the confusion, and the whole room is watching us. I must not stomp on her beliefs, I must instead step softly around them, and try to speak to the tender insides of most of us that want to choose love, and connection, and acceptance. I am tasked with making her believe, even for just a second, that her God would never make her choose between her faith and the humanity and rights of any of his creations to peacefully exist. It is not important to me in those few seconds that everyone in the room agrees with me, but it is vital that they witness her allowing her heart to stretch open enough to make even the possibility of room for people like me. To do this I have to make the tiny terrified teenager that still lives inside of me believe that nobody's God hates me, and that it is really only humans that are capable of twisting faith into hate.

I woke up this morning to the news that Trump has passed a new law allowing homeless shelters to refuse to house transgender people, and a memo from his administration was leaked to the media that includes instructions on how to spot transgender women to target them for discrimination. The memo says homeless shelters can use "factors such as height, the presence (but not the absence) of facial hair, the presence of an Adam's apple" to find suspected trans women.

Right below that news was another article about how the University of Maryland St. Joseph Medical Center is being sued after refusing to treat a transgender man. The facility defended its decision, stating it was following the Ethical and Religious Directives for Catholic Health Care Services drawn up by church officials.

There are days when I am simply not capable of making myself believe that I can find the good parts in the hearts of some humans, or their gods. When it comes to using faith as a shield to hide your hate or excuse your bigotry, or give yourself a reason to kill, well I cannot think of a greater sin. I confess I cannot imagine believing in any god that would condone refusing another soul something as simple as shelter or medical care, or an education, for any reason.

I speak to a lot of teachers and teacher candidates, and school staff and administrators as part of the work that I do in schools.

I do this to quiet the murmurings of my own high school hallway ghosts, to sing a lullaby a little louder than my own change-room inspired nightmares and school-bus flashbacks.

I tell a little story about the time I ended up being housed in the men's dormitory at a university in Saskatoon during the same weekend that an evangelical Christian basketball tournament was happening on the very same campus. I joke about imagining pre-top surgery me showering naked in a giant tiled room full of evangelical Christian farm boys from rural Saskatchewan. I do this to illustrate how hard it can be for trans and non-binary people to access things like public schools and places.

I almost always get a letter afterwards. Usually from an evangelical Christian gym teacher, often from Saskatchewan, who takes issue with me drawing any kind of attention to the adversarial relationship between his faith and my people.

I muster up all of the patience and respect that I am able to, and then I ask him who he feels is most responsible for the well-known conflict between his religion and trans people. I ask him what he is doing right now to reconcile this relationship. I ask him if he has reached out to any of his fellow parishioners to support them when their church is telling them they must choose between loving their god and loving their own children.

I always wonder about the queer kids in his gym class. I worry for the trans kids he is teaching. I think about the girls' volleyball team he coaches, and the messages he is leaking into their hearts about who they are, and what they are capable of, and how they should feel about their bodies.

And I question and question again and again why I feel I must always be so careful not to step on his faith, when I am invited to places and specifically asked to speak to and undo the harm his beliefs are capable of doing to every kid he wields his words over. At night in the dark when I cannot sleep, I hope and pray to my own gods and saints that he doesn't have a queer son at home, that he will never have a trans daughter.

And then I promise myself again that I will be there for all of his queer children, that I will show up for all of his trans family, should they ever come to me asking for the love and acceptance that he was unable or unwilling to give them. I will be their cool uncle, the aunt that always just listens without interrupting, I will be their brother who picks them up to drive them to a safer place, their sister who saves their supper in a Tupperware in the fridge for them and lets them do a couple of loads of laundry while they sleep on the couch.

I have read and re-read your letter. I keep stopping to breathe at the bit where you write about the many years you believed that your girl's brain was not capable of doing math. How that belief has wormed its way into your head and still nibbles away in there, to this day.

What I said to that room full of statisticians in Terrace three years and one month and twelve days ago now, is still very true. I want us to build a world where each and every one of us is supported and encouraged to live up to our full and unabridged, unsqueezed, and untrampled human potential.

Did you come to the evening gig that night in the same longhouse? I can't remember if you were there, too, or if you were only in the morning session. Do you remember the logger that stood up that night and confessed to the room that he wrote poetry, and that the pressure to always be a tough guy had hurt him deeply, his whole life, and had even harmed his relationship with his own son? He took off his sweat-stained Caterpillar ball cap and held it in both hands in front of his chest as he spoke, and then apologized for the tears that he could not force to stop from falling. I was reminded again for the ten millionth time how much I believe that we need to dismantle our gender box prisons and free men like him, too, that he has suffered every bit as much as the little boy who always wanted to play the flute and wear tiaras, and the little girl who grew up believing that she couldn't do math.

If there is one wrong thing in this world that I could undo right now it would be to drain away all the shame that we have been taught to feel whenever we cry.

It is not as simple as teaching ourselves to not see crying as weak, or as feminine. I don't want to teach that crying is a show of strength, either. I want us to see tears as a simple by-product of thinking or feeling or listening or speaking to the world around us. I want us to see crying as being inextricably linked to living, like exhaling is to the act of breathing.

I think one of the most valuable things this culture steals from our men is their tears.

I'm so grateful that you were in that room in Terrace that day, Melinda, and that you found things in the stories I told that morning that I didn't even realize were hidden there in my words. I am glad that you have found a place to keep your faith, and your feminism, and your queerness all safe and tucked, intact and together, inside of you. I take heart in that fact, I really do. Thank you for reminding me again of how powerful a story can be, and how much of that power is found inside of the person who is listening, and that that power to transform is not only held or handled by the heart of the one who is doing the telling.

If this world should ever heal itself enough that we are able to gather in large groups one day, and if I am ever lucky enough to be asked to tell stories in a crowded room again, when and if anyone stands up after and asks me a question about that crossroads where their faith and my existence seem to collide, I will think of you, and I will remember your letter, and I will try to find enough room in my heart to keep my faith in all of us.

With much love and respect,
Ivan

10.

DON'T CALL ME BY YOUR DEADNAME

NOVEMBER 29, 2019

Dear Ivan,

When I was I think 13 or 14, me and my mom came to see you tell some stories in Monterey. We drove a few hours to see you and then after your show we went up to talk to you, and I asked you to sign my copy of *One in Every Crowd*. When I told you who to sign it to, you got real quiet and told me that we had the same birth name. I think you could tell by looking at me that I wouldn't be going by that name forever. My mom took a picture of us and I remember how firm your grip on my arm was. It was the same night that you talked, for the first time I believe, about just having top surgery. I dunno if you remember me or this, but I certainly do. I'm writing this to let you know that now I'm 20, had top surgery myself a year and a half ago, I use they/them pronouns, and my name is Leslee.

Your stories mean so much to me. I just finished reading *Rebent Sinner* and loved it by the way. But your stories did a lot for me. "Dear Lady in the Women's Washroom" was I think the first piece of yours I saw, a video of you reading it, and as someone who has been harassed in restrooms for as long as I can remember, it was the first time hearing that I wasn't alone in that. It was the first thing that made my dad really understand why I was always so upset about using the bathroom in public. (He's a great guy btw.) After that I tried to get ahold of as much of your writing as I could find. Your stories helped teach me how to be non-binary, trans, butch, attracted to women, and what someone like me might look like. That I could learn to fit, even a bit uncomfortably sometimes, into my own skin. That I could be strong and gentle and loving. So thank you thank you thank you from the bottom of my heart. If you're ever in California again I really hope to see you perform.

I'm sure you get a lot of emails like this. I don't intend to lay my traumas down at your feet, I'm sure you get a lot of that too. But I hope it's ok if I tell you a little bit about me, maybe tell you a story.

I've got a real supportive family, which I am so thankful for. Turns out my 2 younger sisters are both gay too, we make quite a squad. I've got 8 piercings (hopefully more soon), and 2 tattoos. One of them says "they/them" on my collarbone, and one of them is a tube of lipstick on my ribs, a reminder to always love and support femmes in the community and to remember an old mentor of mine who passed away, in one of those ways I'm sure you're thinking. I also got a denim vest with a buncha buttons and handmade patches. A regular old punk, but I think I clean up nice. I'm studying to be a math teacher right now, but who knows. Partly cause I love math, partly I think I'd be good at it, and largely cause I wanna make high school better for others than it was for me. A lot of the stuff that happened to me and my friends in high school I'm realizing now shouldn't have happened. So maybe I'll be able to help with that.

I also have worked for the past 5 years as a counsellor at a summer day camp for young trans and gender nonconforming kids and their families. I watched it grow from 12 kids the first year, to the 68 we had enrolled last year. We have kids from 4-13 years old, and it's legitimately the best part of my summer, getting to meet these beautiful powerful silly as all fuck kids. I wanted to share some of the stories from there, cause they make me real happy and I think you might enjoy them.

Judith Butler came down one year to interview the kids and us for a book or something. I did an interview with her where I talked about my experiences and we ended up talking about my packer, and I'll never forget that she said, "oh kid, I've been packing since long before you were crawling." She's so cool. Anyway it was water day, which meant we spray all the kids with hoses and have water balloons and a kiddie pool and throw a big old plastic tarp on the grass and slide down it, slip 'n slide style. Eventually we convinced Judith Butler to run down this slip 'n slide, and me and some other counsellors snuck up behind her at the end to dump a big bucket of water all over her. I dunno how many people can say that they've seen one of the most prominent gender theorists slide down a slip 'n slide and then get ambushed by a bunch of trans teenagers with a bucket, but I can.

We were reading a story all together one day, and the character in it talked about wearing her best outfit, so we paused to ask the kids what their best outfit would be. We had a lot of fun responses, but my favourite was from this young girl who said she would want to wear "all leather."

Another good one was when a kid got slime stuck in her hair, because she's a kid and of course she did. My sister, who also works there, worked diligently to get it out. The kids asked her how she could be so good at getting the slime out, and she replied, "well at home I'm a professional slime remover." One of them asked, "wait that's a job?" and my sister said, mostly truthfully, "well almost anything can be a job." And one of the kids, bless her lil heart, shouted back, "I wanna spank people for my job!"

A lot of being a counsellor is really nice, just to get to see these kids enjoy a summer camp. Especially as someone who got called a "he/she" at summer camp, before I even knew what that meant. No matter how hard things are getting at school or what things are like at home, just for a week or two the kids can play around and just be kids. Some of it is more intense though, in all the ways you're probably thinking. Some of it is beautiful, I've had kids come out to me and tell me how cool it was to meet someone like me. They and their parents say I'm a role model, which feels wild because I'm only 20 and also a mess. But it still feels very important to be there for them.

I hope it was alright for me to send this to you. Your work has seriously changed my life. I hope I can be the kind of person who makes my community, all the people who came before me and made this world better for me, and all the people yet to come, proud. Thanks for showing me the kind of person I hope I can become. I hope you're having a really great day!

Sincerely,
Your birth name buddy (deadname dude?)
Leslee

DECEMBER 2, 2019

Hey Leslee:

Thank you for your great letter. It brought a smile to my face in the middle of this swamp of email I am trying to catch up on, and this grey and rainy Vancouver day. I will keep it and re-read it on the hard days.

I wish you the very best in your good work with the kids. It sounds to me like you are already well on your way to being a great role model. Knowing that most of us are often a mess is step one, I have come to believe.

Thank you so much for writing. I'm glad my stories bring you some sense of community and reflection. This is, for me, the greatest compliment ever.

love your birth name buddy,
Ivan

Dear Ivan,

Thank you so much for replying!! It means a lot that you liked my email and that you had the time to answer. I've tried to reply to it a couple times but I always got real worried about what to say. I was real sick for the last few months, with mono, that I didn't even get from kissing anyone which would have been a good story, and I've been reading a bunch. My mom, who says hi by the way, got me *Tomboy Survival Guide* and it's been amazing to read. I remember when I was a kid and a teen and I thought I was the only one. I'm sad so many of us think that but even now, with 3 trans roommates, it's good to read about you and your life and remember what it was like when I thought I was alone, and how I really wasn't. Though it did make me freak out for a second about whether my nipples were swapped lmao. I also read *Stone Butch Blues* for the first time, which was a transformative experience. It felt like the first time I watched any of your poetry.

I'm all hunkered down right now, cause of the virus and everything. We all work in food service and are essential services but my roommate is immunocompromised so we're not going out at all to keep him safe. Luckily we have sick pay. I hope you're safe and doing well! If you're ever in California again doing performances or anything I'll do my best to make it. Hope you're good, or at least ok given the current everything.

Your birth name buddy,
Leslee

JULY 26, 2020

Dear Leslee:

Thank you for your email. Please say hi back to your Mom for me.

Last December I wrote you a short response to your letter. Now, it's July, and the world has both slowed down and somehow sped up all at the same time, and everything has changed. I'm sitting down to write you the response I wish I had had the time to give you way back in December.

I'm going to start with taking a couple of minutes to be grateful for moms like yours. Those moms that will take the time to drive for several hours all the way to Monterey Bay to take their 13-year-old kid to see some writer reading stories on a stage in a dusty auditorium on a college campus. I do remember meeting you both, even though that was seven years ago now, almost to the day. I remember all those tall glass windows in the foyer next to the book table, that terrible carpet under our feet. If I remember correctly, didn't we talk about the styley plaid short-sleeved shirt you were wearing that night? I'm pretty sure we did.

I meet quite a few moms like yours, and I meet quite a few 13-year-olds that resemble that kid you were back in 2013, and I truly believe this makes me a very lucky person.

I know it's kind of a cliché to say that it is getting letters like yours that keeps my foot on the gas and my feet in my boots and my eyes on the yellow lines when the road gets rough, but that doesn't make it any less true for me.

Sometimes I wish I could magically contact every 13-year-old trans or non-binary kid that I have ever met over the last two decades of road, and gather us all together somewhere so that we could all see just how not alone we really are. So we could all see and believe in each other. Turn that army of lonely into the best party any of us have ever been to.

I think it was later that same night that you and I met that I went swimming for the first time since having my top surgery. I wish I could bottle that feeling of water running over my brand-new chest, and take a sip of it whenever I'm scared of doing something that involves change, or pain, or facing down something unknown.

I just read your letter again, and then scrolled through Twitter for a minute while the kettle boiled, only to find that the Famous Author of Wizard Books has penned a third transphobic rant to her 14 million followers, once again claiming that Innocent Children are being forced into unwanted surgery or hormone blockers by the Evil Trans Lobby.

It makes me wonder if she has ever met and really listened to a kid like the one I met in that theatre in Monterey Bay back in 2013. Makes me wonder if she really cares about the kid I once was.

Between the two of us, we could tell her ten thousand stories about all the times we were scared to be in a public washroom, and how it wasn't trans people hassling us in there, it was people who look and talk a lot like her.

I wish she would listen to our stories of how we came to find ourselves, how we fought the lonely and the fear and the forced conformity and found ourselves, without a roadmap, without a mirror, and with most of the world still screaming in our ears that we don't even exist.

Thank you for sharing some of your stories about teaching at the youth camp.

I remember the first queer youth camp I worked at, in Alberta in 2007. Alberta is one of the most conservative provinces in Canada, in nearly every sense of the word, and there were kids who had travelled to be there from all over the region. I remember watching the youth file into the cafeteria on that first day, from places with names like Canmore and Fort Smith and Moose Jaw and High Level. Kids who were so used to being the only one at school were now magically the majority, if only for those four glorious summer days in Edmonton. I remember the talent show on the last night, watching the shy, long-eyelashed kid from a small reserve up north do the full-on splits onstage to a Lady Gaga song while fifty brand new friends sang along to every word and exploded with joy at the end. I remember hoping for some version of that for all of us.

I also really appreciated the image of Judith Butler on a slip 'n slide. Maybe I will try to keep that story in my head the next time I try to read all of *Gender Trouble* without getting lost and giving up.

Here is the thing about role models that I have learned from you, Leslee: I need you just as much as you need me. Ours is a symbiotic relationship, where we trade strength and hope and bravery back and forth, and I am so grateful for these words and stories that continue to string us together. I'm glad you found a skin that fits you. I'm blessed to be able to create art that brings people like you into my life. It's a great and cosmic circle that keeps me breathing and believing and writing.

I don't know when I will make it back to California. I was supposed to do a gig in Santa Monica in the middle of May, but it was cancelled, and it doesn't look like the border that separates us will open any time soon. Google tells me there are over ten thousand new cases in your state today, alone. I hope you and your roommates are still able to mostly stay home, and keep relatively healthy. I think of you, and your roommates, and your essential-service jobs in food service, whenever someone writes yet another half-researched article or tweets a clueless comment about why infection rates are on the rise in the youth population. Who exactly do they think is flipping their burger and pouring that beer that they are enjoying on that restaurant patio?

Please, please stay as safe as you can and keep in touch,

your friend,
Ivan

II.

AND THE WATER

Hi Ivan! This is Lynne, Bernie's partner. I realized that I don't think I ever reached out to you after my top surgery . . . I ended up going full speed ahead in the private sector and booked it with Garramone in late January 2018. I just couldn't bear to wait any longer and had a credit line that allowed me to do it. So I just celebrated two years post and am doing great. It was the best thing I've done for myself and couldn't be happier. Just wanted to say thank you for your support and for the time you took to talk me through things. And also for being the inspiration that made this 45 year old to take the leap! Hope storytelling life is treating you well. Keep them coming. Xx

Dear Lynne:

Thank you for your message. You sent it on February 25. I was sitting in the driver's seat in my car in the parking lot of a motel in Nanaimo when I first read it.

I do that a lot, read my emails and messages while sitting in my car after I park it. In my old truck the engine used to make a ticking sound as it cooled, but my new car is pretty quiet. I do this at home sometimes, too, just sit there for a while in my car in the underground parking lot under my building, waiting for the song on the radio to finish, or the podcast I'm listening to to wrap up, and I almost always do this when I first arrive somewhere when I'm on the road for work. When I'm away from my apartment too much my car becomes like my surrogate portable couch, or my travelling kitchen table, more like home to me than another hotel room, an unfamiliar restaurant.

So I sat in my car last February, next to the swish and thrum of rush hour traffic on the island highway, and I read your message, the 6 o'clock CBC news on the radio in the background and the rain falling blurry on my windshield.

Happy two-year noboobiversary, Lynne. I just passed my seven-year mark, this last June 3, and I agree, it was the single best thing I've ever done for myself. It still feels like a tiny private miracle to me every morning when I slip just a tshirt on over my head and barefoot it downstairs to put the kettle on for coffee and let the dog out for a pee. No binder, no bra, no tape. Just my shirt against my skin. Every day now for the last seven years.

I've always loved swimming, as far back as I can remember. My mom said I was never afraid of the water, even as a toddler. I can remember my dad holding me horizontal while I dog-paddled in the sandy shallow bit of McClintock Bay back home in Marsh Lake, next to the Dugases' long sun-bleached dock, the waves rocking the bows of the beached canoe and little fibreglass rowboat tied to the thicket of poplar trees that arched over the water there.

We always had a boat, even before my dad learned to build them with his own hands and tools out of aluminum, and I spent most of my summers in and around the water.

I caught fish and tadpoles and chased frogs and followed those long-legged water bugs along the shoreline. I collected rocks and built driftwood lean-tos on the hot sand. My mom used to suntan on shore, looking up from the Stephen King or Robert Ludlum book in her lap and shading her eyes with her right hand to count heads and make sure all of the kids were still floating okay. She used to make us come out of the water when our lips started to turn blue and wouldn't let us back in until the pads of our fingertips weren't puckered and shrivelled anymore.

I remember the summer she started making me wear a tshirt. I think I was about ten. It was years before my nipples started to itch and grow harder there, but still, she insisted. Cover yourself up, she would say. You're too old for that now. Come over here and put this on, I'm not going to tell you again.

My pasty little flat chest looked just like my little sister's, just like my boy cousins' did. I was taught to hide my breasts long before I had them.

I don't remember ever wanting them to grow, or wishing they were bigger, even though I was mercilessly teased about how small they were all throughout high school.

I played hockey on a boys' team in my hometown until I was sixteen. I was the only girl playing in the entire territory back then, in the

80s. There were parents and members of the hockey community in Whitehorse that did everything they could to try to squeeze me out of the league. They pointed out that the regulations stated that I wasn't permitted on the ice without a cup to cover my groin, and without shoulder pads that covered my breasts. My mom foiled these attempts by calling a specialty hockey supply store, all the way down south in Vancouver, and getting a girl's groin protector and women's shoulder pads shipped up on the Greyhound bus. Once again, I was made to cover up and protect breasts that I didn't even have yet.

I think in some ways I learned to hate them before I had them. I successfully swallowed the message that they were shameful, and a strange and unspoken liability.

I spent all of my early twenties wearing a too-tight tank top, a tshirt, a long-sleeved shirt and a jacket. I could live with them hidden under all of those layers. Then came the elastic bandages, then the binder, then the compression shirt.

I quit swimming in public pools in my early thirties. My breasts were too big by then, and I just couldn't squeeze me and my gender identity into a woman's swimsuit anymore. I just couldn't. I would look at black-and-white pictures of men in striped full-body swimsuits circa 1920 and dream of diving boards and the smell of chlorine, but I quit swimming in pools for about 15 years or so. I would still skinny dip in rivers, or wear shorts and a tshirt to jump in the lake, but I always felt all eyes were directed at my chest, and I could not find that place inside of me that felt weightless in the water anymore.

Sometimes now when I read the stuff that TERFs say online about doctors and the trans lobby forcing confused kids onto hormones and into surgeries, well, I almost cannot contain my rage. If they actually had one clue what it is like for us? When I think back about how I had to explain repeatedly that in every picture I held in my head of myself I had a flat chest, first to my doctor, then to the counsellor, then that psychologist, then the psychiatrist, and finally, three years later, the surgeon. When I think about how I bound down those bigger and then bigger unloved breasts for nineteen years, until I started to lose the feeling in three fingers on my left hand, and just could not face another sweaty summer never being able to take a full and deep breath unless I was at home alone and naked in a room with no mirrors in it. How I had to sweat through three more summers after that, anyway, waiting to get my surgery date scheduled in. Who is it exactly who could argue against anyone else getting the medical help that they need?

Even now, seven years free of them, trying to find the words to describe what it feels like to have my own blood pumping into, and my own skin covering, a part of me that has never really been a part of me? I cannot even bring myself to think about what my relationship to my body could have been like all of those years, had I felt like I had the option to have top surgery when I was 18, instead of 44 years old.

Instead I remind myself what it felt like to swim that first time seven summers ago, the skin of my new chest still pink and scarred and tender, and my heart so big with relief that I thought it might split my ribcage and escape into the water and swim all on its own alongside of me. I broke into a closed swimming pool with two other writers one late July night, we slid a maxed-out credit card into the lock on the gate and slipped inside the fence and we skinny dipped, brown skin and wrinkled skin and reborn skin together under a nearly full moon in a California sky.

Every time I get a letter from someone asking me about top surgery, I want to tell them forty-four stories about swimming. I want to tell them how I never miss the feeling in my nipples as much as the whole rest of me missed the water all of those years.

The other day I was driving, and I felt it again, felt it flare from under my seat belt. That kind of like a bee sting burning where I usually feel the nothing in my nipples now. That almost hurt of the nerves there knitting themselves back together, still, seven years later and cell by cell, the skin there is waking up and I can feel the swish of my shirt, the rub of the seat belt, the tips of her fingers, the sun.

And the water.

I got another letter last night from an older butch, asking me if I think she is too old now for top surgery.

So I sat down to write you this letter first.

I'm so glad 45-year-old you took that leap. I'm glad we talked on the phone that night, me stretched out on my couch in Vancouver, and you and all of your questions calling me from Montreal. I'm honoured that you felt like you could come to me with your wondering.

I will think of you tomorrow morning when I pull my shirt on and take the dog out to pee and then pack a lunch and load the cooler into the car.

Because tomorrow is Friday, and we are going swimming.

with much love and solidarity,
Ivan

12.

DISTINGUISHED
LECTURE

Hello Ivan—

I attended your lecture last night . . . It was so wonderful. Quite distinguished in my humble estimation. I really appreciate your perspective on growing up working class. Your story is very close to mine . . .

My father was a storyteller. My favorite memories of my father are of him sitting around the campfire telling a story with a look of joy on his face in remembering some past humorous event. In some way, many storytellers seem to share an intonation of voice . . . a way of speaking. So when you speak, it reminds me of him. I am also reminded of him when you tell stories about your father. The beauty of their gruff masculinity and the vulnerability that's there under the surface. It makes me so happy to hear you tell stories about him . . . even the short little comments about his thoughts/advice. It invariably makes me tear up . . . but since I am in a public place and it doesn't make much sense to others as to why I am crying, I gulp back my tears. But when I read your stories about your dad, I sob like a babe!

Speaking of my father in the past tense suggests he's dead. He's not. He and my mum live in Moorhead, Minnesota (across the river from Fargo, North Dakota) in the same house I grew up in. But for over two years, they haven't spoken to me and have responded to my emails with only a line of "hope you are well." I came out to them when I was 16. I made my father cry (the only time in my life I ever saw him cry— not even at his parents' deaths) and I went on to date men and to marry a wonderful man whom I am still close friends with. At the end of my marriage two years ago, I came out to them again. They explained that they would continue to see and speak to me if I never talked about "that" and never brought any of those "people" to their house. Despite missing them, I choose not to hide myself.

Why I am telling you this? I sort of wonder myself. But I have felt a great desire to tell you about this for a while. But I feel so "star struck" that I cannot bring myself to talk to you. Also I'd likely cry and not be able to say anything! I want to share my gratitude for what a wonderful gift you give me with the stories you write/tell about your father and family. It's a smidge of my own. It helps me remember that which I actively avoid thinking about due to my sadness and disappointment.

So thank you, Ivan Coyote, for allowing me to be with you and your dad. Allowing me to be with my own.

Sincerely,
Angela

Dear Angela:

I want to thank you again for your email. I can see from my email history that I wrote you a short response thanking you for your letter four days after I received your original email, way back in 2011. It's probably going to be weird hearing back from me now, very nearly nine and a half years later, but I always meant to write you a true and proper response, so here I am.

I talked to my dad today. I called him just before I sat down to write to you.

Have you ever heard the song "Mercy Now" by Mary Gauthier? It's the first verse of that song that always reaches right into my chest and squeezes so hard:

My father could use a little mercy now
The fruits of his labor
Fall and rot slowly on the ground
His work is almost over
It won't be long and he won't be around
I love my father, and he could use some mercy now

I was driving north in my old truck the first time I really listened to those lyrics. The Alaska Highway. I've lost count of how many times I've spent four days alone on that road, a mug full of coffee between my thighs and a sad song on the stereo, and the road stretched out like a dusty zipper through all of those spruce and pine trees. I'm always either on my way to see my family, or on my way back to the big city, and processing my visit with them. This time it was early August, in 2010, and I was on my way to the Yukon for a few weeks of fishing and family and recharging. My last gig before I hit the road was a music festival on Vancouver Island, and I heard Mary play twice over that past weekend. I bought three of her CDs and stashed them in the glove compartment. On day two, somewhere just past Prince George, I heard those lines of hers, and that song rarely left my head for days afterwards.

My dad lives in a little town called Atlin, about 200 kilometres south of Whitehorse, just over the Yukon-BC border. Wikipedia tells me it has about 450 full-time residents, and that seems about right to me. He lives just off of Warm Bay Road, about five clicks from the little gas station and grocery store/post office/liquor store on the main road that runs downhill through town to the big lake. The name Atlin comes from the Tlingit word *Áa Tlein*, which means "big body of water."

Every time I turn left off of the road to Whitehorse, and then right, and then left and left again into his willow-lined driveway, I hear Mary Gauthier's lyrics in my head. The fruits of his labours fall and rot slowly on the ground. I can picture his little house right now. He never finished painting the railing on the deck. The lawn hasn't been mowed since I did it last fall before I left. His boat is still in the garage, its engine sitting in pieces on a tarp on the concrete floor of his shop, even though it's almost August now. He's sitting in his chair on the corner of the wraparound deck, smoking a cigarette. He will wave when I drive up and park, but he won't get up. His feet hurt and so does his back.

I spent all of last summer there. He and I were supposed to work together fixing up his place, finishing the sauna he started the previous fall, and building a little cabin out in the trees behind his place for me and Sarah. We had big plans. But the red wine and the depression got to him before I could, and he spent most of the summer smoking on that deck.

I got the roof repairs on his place done, and cleaned up the property, took load after load of stuff to the dump, finished the sauna, and got the foundation and the sub floor for the little cabin built. My cousin Levon, fresh out of carpentry school, came and helped me out with the cabin.

I remember one morning when I came into his house from my little travel trailer to put on some coffee and make oatmeal. My dad had the television on, but the sound turned right down. He was sitting on the couch wearing the same clothes he'd had on the day before, watching me with watery eyes as I moved around his kitchen. He sighed and stared at the rug on the floor in front of the couch. Told me he was sorry he hadn't been any help with stuff around the place lately.

"I just haven't been myself ever since Pat died," he confessed. "I know it's been three years now, and I should just get the fuck over it and get on with my life, but I can't seem to do that."

I walked over and took his empty coffee cup from the end table and refilled it, dropped in two sugar cubes and passed it to him.

"Dad," I told him softly. "Pat died six years ago now, not three."

Anyway.

I just read your letter again. I won't pretend that I can understand at all what it must be like to be so disconnected from your parents. I'm sorry for the pain that this brings you. I'm so glad hearing my stories about my dad helps you with that sadness, even just a little.

I'm not sure if the truth of him and I will bring you any comfort, either, but I feel compelled for some reason to tell you that my relationship with my father is by far the most painful and complicated one in my life, bar none, no contest, and since forever.

I know he lies to me about how much he is drinking. I know he lies to me about whether or not he drank before he drove that long and winding highway from Whitehorse back to Atlin alone. I'm not even sure anymore why I ask him these kinds of questions.

I have prayed for him to get or stay sober for well over thirty years now, ever since him and my mom divorced, and the booze really took the wheel in his life. If he was a happy (or even a happier) drunk I think I could let it go, for the most part, but he is not.

My sober father is funny and talented and creative and hard-working and charismatic. He loves dogs and talking to strangers in the grocery store and cooking and fishing and building boats.

My drunk father is cynical, mistrusting, paranoid. He's angry, guilty, unemployed, and depressed. He loves nothing. But mostly, he is just so sad.

I'm not sure what would be worse, to be honest, not talking to him at all and wondering if he is okay, or, talking to him every Saturday like I do, and knowing for certain that he is not.

I've never been one to quantify pain. I don't think sadness can be measured.

I read your letter again, and this time I learned that sometimes I tell the good stories about my father to strangers at shows so that I can remember him telling a joke, and teaching me to tie the right knot in my fishing line. I choose the stories I tell about him so that I can remember him younger, and handsome, and laughing. I tell good stories so that those are the words that ring out louder in the room than my heartbreak and my disappointment do.

Nine and a half years is a long time to wait for a letter to come. I think if I had written you back properly way back then, this might be a very different letter. Nine years ago my dad's wife was still working in town at the auto parts place. She was about to retire and we didn't know anything about the cancer in her throat, or her lungs, or her brain. Nine years ago I didn't have any grey hair yet, and I hadn't been married, or divorced. Nine years ago my father's boat was still tied up at the dock in that big lake, ready for the weekend to come, and he mowed the lawn once a week all summer.

Nine years ago you hadn't really talked to your parents for two years.

I would love to hear back from you about how things are with your parents now, if things have shifted, or grown, or grown over. I don't think that the guy who wrote that time heals all wounds had a dad anything like yours, or mine.

I hope these last nine years have brought you a little more peace in your heart. I hope you have found and held on to some good stories of your father, too. Maybe he grew tired of missing you, too, and came around a little. If life has been kind, maybe you took your girlfriend home to Moorhead, Minnesota for a visit last winter, and your parents cooked a roast and put out the good tablecloth and the new silverware. Maybe you and your dad lit a big fire after dinner and you all sat around it together, just talking.

Storytellers. We can't help but keep hoping that there might just be a happier ending in there, somewhere.

Please say hi to Winnipeg for me.

With much love,
Ivan

13.

TWO KINDS OF BLUE

This next letter came to me in the form of a handwritten note I found tucked under the windshield of my car after a gig I did at the Belfry Theatre in Victoria, on May 29, 2019. The words were scrawled and squished onto the back of a flyer, in two very different colours of blue ink. It was raining a little by the time I finished at the book signing table and packed up my gear and got back to my car. At first I didn't even see the note, it was late, and I was post-show tired. My windshield wipers squeaked it back and forth in the dark, and I got out to remove it so I could drive away safely. I assumed it was a flyer for a local pizza place or something like that, and I almost just crumpled it up, but then I saw the now-blurry blue ink on the back. I smoothed it out, tucked it into my jacket pocket, and brought it back to my hotel room and dried it out on the bathroom counter next to the sink. I'm glad I did, because it was a good one. I don't know who wrote this note, but I've included this transcription, and my undeliverable-by-normal-methods response to this beautiful note, because I believe that the power of writing and stories will help my dispatch find its way back to the anonymous note-leaver.

Ivan,

I bought a book after the show but standing in line to tell you a sad story about my dad dying of AIDS in the St. Paul's palliative ward the year after your photo, or saying that I too love Rae Spoon, all of that doesn't mean too much standing in a line full of strangers waiting for a signature and to tell you how fantastic were, are and will always be (and how much do you appreciate run-on sentences?)

Well, I'm the kind of person that quietly leaves notes saying how much you touched us, how much you are the story of triumph that I want to hear more of.

S.

AUGUST 23, 2020

Dear S.:

My first question when I got back to my hotel room that night was why was your note written in two very different colours of blue ink? Did your pen run out halfway through writing it, and you had to stop, standing in the spitting rain under the streetlights, and dig around in your backpack for another?

It's late August now, about fourteen months later, and the second colour of blue ink has faded to a light purple. I dried your note out that night and took it home and tucked it into a file folder. I knew that one day I would flip through that folder and pull out your note and write you back, even though I don't yet know where to send this letter, so I will have to rely on happenstance and hope that these words of mine find their way into a book, and that book will eventually meander its way back to you somehow.

My second question is, how did you know which car was mine? Which windshield wiper your note belonged under? I suspect that you were one of the two people I had talked to earlier that night, before the show, about whether or not I would get towed if I took a chance and parked in the lot behind the theatre, or in that strip of numbered spots behind the old apartment building. I finally found that spot across the street and up the road a little, and you saw me park my car there. It had to be you. You were wearing a backpack and had a wallet chain swinging against your right hip, and big black boots. I'm almost certain you are the mysterious note-leaver, and I'm pretty sure that backpack had at least two blue pens in the outside pocket.

I have always liked a good mystery.

I'm sorry that you lost your father to AIDS. If you are indeed the person I talked to before the show that night, you must have been very young when he died. Younger than I was back in 1990, anyway. It must have been hard to lose your dad to AIDS when you were just a kid. There was still so much stigma and fear floating around in the air back then. It breaks my heart to imagine little you having to navigate your way through all of that, fatherless and grieving.

Yours is not the first letter I've received about that story. Some stories have longer legs than others, it seems, and that story has walked farther than I could ever have imagined it might. Some stories shake other stories out of the chests of almost everyone who hears them, and I guess it should be no surprise that telling a story of my loved ones lost to AIDS would call forth a multitude of ghosts from so many queer hearts.

I'm going to tell you another story, one I've never told anyone before, ever. It's a story some members of my family will not like me telling, but for some reason I think it belongs in this sort of unsendable letter back to you, so I'm finally going to tell it.

My grandmother Pat had an older brother named John Francis. Everybody called him Jack. He was tall and handsome and smart. He was an airplane pilot. He learned to fly during the Second World War, and then became a commercial airline pilot after the war was over. He flew for Air Canada for many years and when he retired in the late seventies, he moved up to the Yukon to be closer to his favourite sister. I loved him a lot. He didn't like kids much, but he liked me, mostly because I was kind of a strange kid. A loner. A reader. A neat freak, like he was. We both had the same favourite dinner: roast chicken drumsticks. We both loved corn on the cob, and maple walnut ice cream. He had a giant record collection and a fancy Bang & Olufsen stereo that absolutely no one but him was allowed to even think about touching.

Until that day when he hired me to come help him clean his windows.

He and I were alone at his rented house a block away from my grandmother's place with our shirtsleeves rolled up and the stereo on. White vinegar and old newspaper did the job for windows according to him. The Janis Joplin record skipped while she was singing about Bobby McGee, and he stopped working and showed me how to squirt the record-cleaning solution onto the vinyl and carefully clean it with the half-round velvet brush, and how to gently lower the needle onto the right groove, and made me swear to never tell anyone he let me put a record on all by myself.

He taught me how to solder, too, and we built a radio from a kit together. He made me listen to the six o'clock news on the CBC radio and would quiz me after about what was the name of our prime minister and the official leader of the opposition, and tell me how important it was to care about world events and to be a critical thinker. He took me and my dog Buck camping to the Atlin warm springs and we ate steak three nights in a row and he let me sleep alone in the grass outside of his travel trailer and gave me a book about identifying constellations that he had had since he was a little boy, back in Saskatoon. He was an excellent whistler. He invented and patented things. He was my great-uncle, but to me he was like a grandfather, except better, because he wasn't a drunk, and he didn't beat up my grandmothers like my actual grandfathers both did.

He got very sick in the early eighties. Kidney failure. There was no dialysis machine in the Yukon, so he had to fly down to Vancouver for treatment. He got many plasma transfusions while in the hospital. St. Paul's, in the West End of Vancouver. He died the night I finished my last final exam of my first year at Capilano College, in late April of 1987. It wasn't until years later all the pieces started to click together to become this story I am finally telling you now. The pneumonia. The little scabby sore on his neck, and the other one on his earlobe, that just wouldn't heal. Was it Kaposi's sarcoma? They wouldn't have tested a heterosexual man in his seventies for HIV, not in 1987. He was already so sick from the kidney failure. They wouldn't have suspected that it was AIDS, not with him, not at that time. The doctors were still blinded by homophobia, and stereotypes. He would have slipped through all of those many deep and wide cracks in the system back then.

I think I lost my great-uncle Jack to kidney failure and AIDS. He died in the very same hospital where you lost your father, and where, a couple of years later, I would go on to lose so many of my beautiful new brothers in the struggle.

I'm not sure why I feel like your note and this story belong together. I just do.

I hope you found other good men to adopt as heart fathers after your father died. I hope they loved you and showed you the stuff fathers are meant to show their kids how to do. I hope you had an Uncle Jack.

I hope next time our paths cross you introduce yourself. I hope this letter grows long legs and walks onto a page that meets your eyes one day, and you know that I found your soggy note that night, and that it is still tucked into the pocket of my laptop sleeve, the new one I got for this new computer that I am typing on right now.

Thank you for writing me, S. I will forever carry at least two pens in my backpack in your honour.

Much love,
Ivan

14.

THEN THERE
WAS THIS
ONE TIME

Hi, Ivan—I was one of the people at the talk you gave at Vancouver General Hospital about trans issues and health care. I'm a trans man who's currently also studying at UBC to become a nurse.

Great talk! I had never heard you speak before, and though I had assumed you'd be funny (knowing some of your writing), I was actually quite relieved to find you angry and unabashedly emotional as well. Somehow, it made me trust more your capacity to represent "us." I was particularly grateful for your repeated comment about how different every trans person's trajectory is, and that it's not always about a journey from one solidified idea of gender to another solidified idea of a gender.

For myself (maybe 5 years older than you?) I finally capitulated (as I really view it) to the gender binarism and transitioned with hormones and surgery only a few years back. It has been both an enormous relief and a real loss in a range of ways—though overall, certainly an improvement in my life & relationships. I was working as a carpenter and becoming a "man" sure made a difference in that respect, too. But I am very interested in people who choose not to capitulate to the binarism and who ask for non-he/she pronouns. I got too tired at long last to keep at it, myself (bathrooms). I crave the stories of people who've made your choice—and I'm especially greedy to know how to be effective as a nurse in regard to the huge variety of genders of people I might encounter in my career. I was very glad to hear your story.

One last thing: about the stress levels you mentioned: my therapist once told me that they measured cortisol levels in trans people and compared them to values for soldiers in combat (in combat!) and found that trans people had higher cortisol levels. Like, really. I thought of mentioning that at VGH during the Q&A period afterward, but didn't want to become a kind of competing voice of trans experience, when people were clearly very taken (and well informed) by yours.

Oh—by the way: you've also made me terrified to fly anywhere. My own particular issues have especially been with passport services, but your knowledge of recent surveillance strategies was a freakin' eye-opener.

Thanks again, man—
very impressive.
Darach

Dear Darach:

Well thank you brother, really, sometimes I'm terrified up there, you know? I can't possibly speak for every one of us, there is no "right language" or perfect Band-aid, and people want all that and more from a 90-minute talk. I just wanted to put my experience out there as a place to start asking questions from, so I am really glad to hear I didn't let you down.

Don't let the airport shit scare you too bad. You get a pat-down, it's pretty intense but for the most part just humiliating. I don't pack through security, and if they pay too much attention to your lack of a penis, you could try my friend's line: "If you are looking for that it's in my carry-on."

I am really interested in the combat situation statistic. I would love the details on where your therapist got the stat from, because I would love to use the detail in similar talks but will then be asked by the academics immediately what the source is. Any idea?

Best of luck with the rest of your school. Always glad to know another one of us is out there on the front lines. That can only be a good thing for everybody. Important work, so thank you for doing it.

best,
Ivan

MARCH 24, 2015

Hi, Ivan—Thanks for the prompt reply. I really want to look into the question of the cortisol info myself, so will try to find out. I'll let you know if I can figure it out.

Thanks again,
Darach

Dear Darach:

That would be great. It's an important number to get out there if we can prove it beyond word of mouth. I fully believe it, but have to have the source to quote it and be taken seriously, you know?

Hi, Ivan—Just a follow-up re: the question of stress hormone levels in trans people: I don't think the research actually exists. I contacted the person who'd originally mentioned the research to me, and it turned out the article only looked at LGB. No T—because trans people taking hormones meant inaccurate measurements of cortisol levels and therefore weren't good test subjects. Mini-rant:

In the scientific world—I genuinely start to believe—there ARE no trans* or gender variant people who aren't on hormones trying desperately to cut off pieces of themselves in order to squeeze back into the gender binarism. So there is absolutely no research in a medical vein about transgender people who have not transitioned in the most conventional sense. Trans people's only relevance to medical science is the transitioning process: it's like, trans folk don't even get colds or something!

There IS research demonstrating that cortisol levels drop once trans people start hormone therapy, our cortisol levels having been above normal before that (but no more detail about just how high above normal). ("Hormonal treatment reduces psychobiological distress in gender identity disorder, independently of the attachment style" —M Colizzi, R. Costa, V. Pace, and O. Todarello, in the *Journal of Sexual Medicine*, January 2013.)

But there is no medical recognition of trans people who only want surgery or hormones, not both, or who aren't modifying their bodies in either way. Hence, research on people who haven't/aren't going to fit themselves into conventional gender categories just doesn't exist—who knows what their cortisol levels are?

All to give more evidence for the "need" for the stress levels you mentioned in your talk—who wouldn't be stressed when they're continually told that they either don't exist, can't exist, or don't merit talking about? But of course no direct evidence because of exactly the same.

Sorry not to be more helpful,

Darach

Dear Darach:

Five years and five months ago today I read your last email to me, and then filed the exchange away in my special letters box in my Gmail, and here we are. The last several months I've been metaphorically dusting off all of those letters, and responding. I owe you an email.

If all went as you were planning back in 2015, you are working as a nurse now. You are one of the many trans nurses I know, and hence you have been on my mind a lot ever since the pandemic started. We "met" at VGH in Vancouver, so that is where I have been imagining you working, for some reason, although I realize we met at a school function for you, and you might have ended up working anywhere in the city or beyond, but in my mind I see you parking a medium-sized blue car in the parking lot outside of VGH. I imagine you in baby-blue scrubs and those white shoes nurses wear, your ID tag on a lanyard around your neck and one Pilot Fineliner pen clipped into your shirt pocket, black ink.

This is just how my brain works.

Anyway, I imagine you right now listening to the end of your podcast on the car stereo, just for a minute, because you always get to work a little early. You have both of your hands on the steering wheel still, even though you are parked, and the engine is off. It's a fucking pandemic and you are a nurse. You have pimples where your mask meets your close-trimmed beard (I heard this from another nurse friend of mine) and a rash on your knuckles from hand sanitizer and sweating in gloved hands. Work has been really hard lately. You have four more minutes.

I wonder who you haven't been able to see since March because of your job, and whether or not you live alone.

I just re-read our emails back and forth several times. There is so much I want us to talk about. You said you were maybe 5 years older than me, and our last correspondence happened five years ago, so that means I am the same age now that you were when you wrote to me.

I'm 51. I wonder, do your feet hurt in the mornings like mine do?

I wonder what made you transition again, from carpenter to nurse? You went from being (as far as your co-workers knew) a woman working as a carpenter, I can only assume with mostly men, to a trans man working in your trade, to a trans man working as a nurse among (as I know from doing multiple gigs for the nurses' union) mostly women.

Damn. We should download what you have probably learned about gender and the binary and socialization from that experience. Fuck that *Men Are From Mars* nonsense, I bet you have the real inside scoop on all of it.

Do we know each other well enough yet for me to tease you about how you still put two spaces after a period, even in 2015, even in an email? Did you learn that in your version of Miss Pruden's typing class back in grade 10 in 1980, like I did in 1985?

Speaking of classes, I'm taking an introductory carpentry course, starting two Mondays from now. The pandemic has cancelled all tours and physical travel for work for me for the foreseeable future, but the upside is, I am finally going to be in one place for long enough to take a class in something. I'm not sure what a socially distanced woodshop is going to look like, but I will find out soon. My partner Sarah and I are building a little cabin way up north, we started last summer with the help of my cousin Levon the carpenter, and got the foundations poured, and the subfloor built, but I'm going to need to expand my skills to continue with it.

Anyway. Where were we? Gender. Stress levels. Cortisol. The medical system. Where we fit, and all the places we do not. Let the research show there is no research. Not on us. In lieu of numbers all we have is our stories. Let me share a couple of stories with you.

For most of my late thirties, and all of my forties, I suffered from extremely heavy periods, some lasting for over 10 days. This is not so uncommon, I know, but the hassle of this was complicated for me because, as you know, I present as pretty masculine, and until the pandemic I was a full-time touring artist, on the road for work an average of about 200 days out of every year. That is a lot of tampons to change in a lot of public washrooms.

I think it was back in 2015 or so, right around when we first met, that I found myself in the Dallas-Fort Worth airport at the very same time another Republican senator was trying to pass one of those bathroom bills that only permits use of the bathroom that corresponds with the gender marker on your birth certificate.

I had long ago decided it was safer (most of the time) to use the men's room in an airport in Texas, even though if that bill passed it would be actually illegal for me to do so. I mean, we were all past security, right? At least no one would have a gun on them in there, I thought. Except the ones in police and security uniforms, of course.

There was one stall in the men's room. The lock was broken. There was no weird tin box in the stall to dispose of my tampon, so I flushed it, even though I have an uncle and a cousin who are plumbers, and I know better. I had blood all over my hands. The dude at the sink next to me notices, says You okay buddy? and then seems confused when all that blood washes off, revealing no visible wound. No scrapes from punching a wall, or cuts from doing manly things. I was afraid to answer him, because my voice might not pass the depth-sounder of your average man from Texas, and so when I said nothing, he narrowed his eyes at me. Took a second, and then a third look. I beat it out of there and tried to disappear into the crowds in the hallway. *Changing my tampon in a public bathroom can literally be a blood sport for me,* I jokingly write into my Twitter app when I get to the departure gate and sit down. I deleted it without hitting send, and put my phone away. It was time to have my identification and gender presentation scrutinized so I could board the airplane and get home.

When I got safely back to Canada, I went in to see my family doctor. Same doctor I had had since 1989, which I know makes me lucky. She knew I was trans, and when I first came out to her, she had educated herself. She never got my pronouns right, but I let it slide because other than that, she was always kind and caring and never called me by my old name, even though I was her patient for twenty-six years before I legally changed it. I told her my periods were getting worse every month. She filled out a referral for me to go to a private ultrasound clinic for an intravaginal MRI, to see if I had fibroid cysts.

The clinic waiting room was packed. The technician walked in, called my name, and I stood up. I was wearing jeans and a button-down shirt, and my hair had just been freshly shorn. Tight fade.

She knitted her eyebrows, glanced at her paperwork, stared over at the woman behind the counter. "Well," she said. "You have made a mistake here." She laughed out loud. "I certainly can't do a vaginal exam on him."

She said this like it was all so very hilarious, and she spoke very loudly, in a packed waiting room. Mostly happy pregnant heterosexual couples getting ultrasounds. They all stared. I froze for a second, and then bolted out of the waiting room, motioning for her to follow me. "Yes," I told her in the hallway by the examination rooms. "That is exactly what I am here for. I'm transgender. That is my private information you just yelled out to everyone. I might not look like it to you, but I have a vagina and it needs an ultrasound."

What followed was the most uncomfortable and humiliating medical procedure I've ever been subjected to. She literally would not touch me. She passed me the lubricated wand and instructed me to put it in myself. She asked me after it was done to sign a consent form, and she admitted I was supposed to have signed before the exam began. She was visibly uncomfortable, curt, and impatient. When it was over she was about to leave. I asked her for a tissue or something to clean myself up, and she took a box of Kleenex off of the counter, tossed it on the exam table at my feet and bolted out of the door. I barely made it back to my truck before the tears came. I sobbed in the parking lot for ten minutes and then called the clinic and asked to speak to the manager. It took days, a three-page email, phone calls and more phone calls, and I finally got a half-assed apology from the someone in charge, and a promise that the technician would be reprimanded. "I don't want her reprimanded," I said, "I want your staff to be educated."

"Do you have any information you can send me?" the manager asked. "Like a one-page sheet, something I can photocopy and just hand out at a staff meeting? We don't really have any kind of budget for this kind of thing."

"Sometimes I just want to go get an intravaginal ultrasound," I tell her. "Sometimes I don't want to turn me taking care of my own health care into your free learning opportunity," I tell her.

She pauses, then asks me to email her the information, which I do, and I never hear back from her again.

I told my doctor about the experience, and she promised me she would also call and complain, and she referred me to a gynecologist, who she assured me was trans friendly.

But first I had to get in to see him. I walked into the office. The woman behind the desk smiled at me and asked me if I was lost. No, I said, I have an appointment with the gynecologist at 8:30. She did a double take, looked uncomfortable, and told me someone would call me in a minute. I waited about 45 minutes. I had to pee, and when I went into the washroom, I got screeched at by an old woman for being in the wrong bathroom.

Finally, a young man called me into the gynecologist's office. He's not the doctor, he explained, he's just going to ask me a few questions. Any chronic health conditions? he asked. Have I ever had a major operation? Yes, I said, I had a double radical mastectomy in 2013. Cancer? He asked. No. I said. I'm trans. He dropped his pen, squirmed in his chair, and really looked at me for the first time. That's okay. He said. I know. I tell him. He looked at the floor, looked at his pen, looked at his papers again. Have you ever had a major operation? he repeated. He was nervous now, and had lost his place in his form.

Something in me snapped. I could almost hear it. I could definitely feel it. It smelled like frustration and it tasted like blood. I realized I'd literally been biting my own tongue.

I'm stopping you here for a minute, I told him. Are you gathering information for the doctor or is this a learning experience for you?

A bit of both, he admitted.

Okay. I said. Here is your learning opportunity for today. I'm done with this. Your homework is to go and educate yourself about the realities of trans people before you conduct yourself like this with another patient. You can take your forms and leave now. I will wait here for the doctor.

Maybe I was too hard on him, I thought, as I waited another 15 minutes for the actual doctor to show up. But it wasn't just him. It was the ultrasound woman, and the front desk woman. And the old woman in the ladies' room. It was the dude in the men's room in Dallas too.

The gynecologist apologized, sort of, for the medical student's conduct. I told him about the woman at the front desk, and the lady in the bathroom too. We have a men's room on this floor, he said. It's just way down the hall and a little hard to find.

But I'm not a man, I told him. And you are supposed to be the trans friendly guy.

I certainly have no problem treating trans people, he said, and I have seen a few of . . . I've seen a couple of trans patients over the years, but predominantly I do pelvic floor reconstructions. My specialty is treating incontinence. He referred me to another colleague of his, and I started all over, waiting another two months, and two long periods to get in to see her.

Great, I thought on my way back to my truck. The woman I scared in the ladies' room was probably incontinent. Good thing she was on her way out when I scared her and she screamed at me, and not on her way in.

Months later, I am finally scheduled for an endometrial ablation. The last thing I hear, just before the general anesthetic kicks in, is one of the staff repeatedly calling me she. The first thing I hear when I wake up is a nurse, also calling me she.

I use the singular they pronoun. I mumble groggily.

What? she says.

I'm trans.

We will worry about that later. She says. Right now, we have more important things to worry about. How much pain are you in? Scale of one to ten.

Depends if you mean physical or emotional, I think, but bite my tongue again, metaphorically.

About a five, I tell the nurse.

Well, we can help you with *that*, she says.

It all turned out to be worth it in the end, though. I had the endometrial ablation and it changed my life, it really did.

I know that by now you have probably heard many stories like these, from multiple trans and non-binary people, and that you most likely have several of your own you are right now packing around with you, but these are just a few of mine.

All this to say how glad I am that you became a nurse. I am tearing up as I write these words, thinking of just how different any of this might have been for me had you been in that ultrasound clinic, that doctor's office, that operating room. What if I had woken up after top surgery, or the ablation, with you standing over me, seeing me for who I really was? Knowing the words I use to describe myself, and using them?

A little thing, some would say. I would not.

The scars on my chest have faded almost totally away, I think my last period arrived late last July, and my old family doctor retired three years ago, but my heart still pounds every time I step into a medical facility of any sort. I often imagine what it must be like for trans people who are not white, or who don't speak English as a first language, or who are not of the masculine variety—how many "tiny little" times are they disrespected, deadnamed, misgendered, disregarded, or refused, while trying to access health care? How many don't even go because they already know?

How many microaggressions are there in a macroaggression? I've always wondered. How do they include us in the death count if the numbers think we don't exist?

Doesn't it all just make your cortisol thrum through your veins just thinking about it? You said in that first email that the measured cortisol levels of trans people were higher than those of soldiers in combat. Maybe you never tracked down the evidence but still, I believe it, because most days it's hard not to feel like we are thrust into a constant battle, just by being. By insisting to exist.

I'm so glad that you exist. I remain ever grateful to know that you are working as a nurse. I think of the million tiny kindnesses I know that you bestow on all of your patients.

Tonight I will light this candle on my desk to keep you safe. It smells like cedar and juniper. It smells like wood. Every time I touch a flame to the wick, it makes me want to build things with my own hands.

Please keep in touch. I love an email, but I'm also old enough to appreciate a good old phone call, too.

With much respect,
Ivan

Hi, Ivan—

I was very pleasantly surprised to get your email—and I enjoyed it a great deal. I know you're a writer, of course, but many authors don't write with the human voice and breath in mind, I feel—where your writing clearly does. Lovely.

I actually have ended up working in a hospital oncology unit. Much cancer treatment these days happens on an out-patient basis, but on our acute-care hospital unit, we have some of the sickest of cancer patients, as well as people getting days-long chemo treatments, and a wide variety of other things. At any one time, one or two may be actively dying, or heading that direction in fairly short order, while others are successfully treated, and move on to the rest of their lives. I wanted to get into nursing for a variety of reasons, but one of them was precisely for this close contact with the deepest mysteries of life: to touch the dying and the dead; to stand face-on to human suffering and admit it into my daily reckonings; to contemplate the human spirit in its extraordinary beauty and appalling self-delusion; and so on. The job has not disappointed in this regard, but I wish I could be clearer to myself what I have really learned from all this. Some friends now seem to view me as the holder of some kind of secret, but I still don't have a clue what it is.

We do wear VGH-style blue scrubs—our Smurf suits, we call them— have done since the start of the coronavirus, so that we aren't wearing our own scrubs to and from work, or laundering them at home. But no blue car: I got rid of my tiny carpentry truck a year ago—one of those little Japanese Tonka toys with the steering wheel on the wrong side—and bought an electric bicycle. I wanted an electric vehicle for environmental reasons, and this was the only one I could afford—and outside of my Tonka-truck years, I've always commuted by bike ever since moving from Saskatchewan almost 35 years ago. My obligatory trans man's beard, unfortunately, is gone—another casualty of coronavirus. N-95s don't work with facial hair, so I shaved it off months ago, and still feel daily regret about it.

As for nursing as a trans person: I was very moved by your stories about living in the liminal world of trans-ness and non-binary-ness. It's true, I have plenty of stories of my own, including in medical situations. I had to have a mammogram once, and had an experience in the waiting room very like yours about getting the ultrasound, for instance. And of course the bathroom stories—an entire genre of trans-specific stories living (and lived) in plain sight, but utterly invisible to the rest of the literary world. But your particular stories still got to me. And I was very flattered by your appreciation of my work as a nurse: very kind of you to say. Though I am really not sure it's deserved.

Because the thing that I'm really torn up about, is that I'm not out as trans at work. I interrogate myself about this every day: I was once a deliberately visible and unapologetic lesbian, and from those days I still believe completely in the political necessity of being out, and visible, and vocal. But somehow I find being out as trans much harder than being out as a lesbian. Part of it is the actual "mechanics" of coming out: it's very easy to talk about "my partner, she . . ." and simply be done with it in just that many words. But I haven't figured out how to come out as trans in such casual terms. "Back when I was a girl . . ." or something similar, doesn't fit into a sentence that can then just roll on to the rest of the intended story. I don't want to stop a conversation in this way; I don't wish to be the focus of the kind of dramatic attention it would draw, either in the moment, or in the ongoing culture of my workplace; I am especially terrified at having my body scrutinized and its detailed gender features parsed out by a bunch of nurses whose eyes are way too attuned to people's physical signs and signals. Coming out as trans feel very much more intimate than being out as a lesbian: it's way too close in.

It seems that I am passing completely at work, and it's convenient to disappear in this way. Sometimes it's even fun to join in the unthinkingly bi-gendered teasing that straight people take for granted: it means I have a place here, and that maybe some of these folks even like me. But it comes at the price of a bizarre ongoing mummery of heterosexual masculinity—not so much in my manner (my dad was a fairly effeminate guy, and I have decided that I'm fine with that as a model for a legitimate version of masculinity), but in the stories the other nurses assume of me. At various points, for instance, I've been directly informed that I must either be a "breast guy" or a "butt guy" (no comment), that if I were kicked in the balls I'd be prostrate with pain, or that I can't find the box of medium chemo gloves in the storeroom because guys can never find things. All said with humour and usually some implied affection. Though there's also the truly offensive stereotype that as a "male" nurse, I am lazy because male nurses always are, even after 5 years of a perfectly solid work ethic on my part.

It is a very odd thing to be the object of this strange double sexism: sexism against my ostensible maleness and all that I therefore automatically embody; let alone my co-workers' complete inability to imagine that perhaps I am not such a "male" at all, and may be something quite else. Even the "female" I once was feels the sting, since all of my female-bodied experience is so utterly erased—periods, breasts, pregnancy and childbirth, living as an ostensible woman in a misogynist world, being the younger sister of two older brothers back in a pre-Second Wave Saskatchewan.

But daily, there is the usual tallying of damage should I come out: some of my workmates would be fine with it, even very positive about it—but my experience since transitioning is that it can also be very surprising who turns out to have a problem with it. Nursing is one of those kinds of work where you have to rely on your co-workers in profound ways; we are extremely close, even while only being colleagues. As a carpenter in a female body, there was the odd guy who was really antagonistic, and I always knew exactly where they were when I leaned over the huge panel saw or stuck my hand into the planer to clear out the woodchips. The dangers as an out trans nurse wouldn't usually be so obvious and physical, but there is still genuine risk, and I am not anxious to go back to living at that level of vigilance. And there's the risk, too, of my being outed by a colleague to the wrong patient—which really could go badly.

Yet I feel quite strongly that I would be a better advocate for my trans/NB patients—of whom I've had a very few—if I were out in my workplace. Your email was a serious reminder of that. I have come out to a couple of my trans/NB patients, but the point of nursing is that my own identity and stories run a distant second place to the needs and meanings of the patients themselves, and I want very much not to insist on their attention to my history unless I think it's of some use to them. I don't know how to say what's important, while leaving all the space to them, to speak their own lives, and fear, and present suffering.

And silence, as a trans person, is an extremely powerful habit to give up very easily. It may begin as an enforced effect of hounding erasure, but for me, it also became an incredibly rich place to live. So badly unspoken when I was young, I am still fiercely driven to be heard, even to my own detriment, but much of my life still resides in this other place. I still experience trans-ness as almost entirely silent. I mean, I can tell stories of how difficult it is to move as trans through a ludicrously cis world, but while those stories communicate some part of what it is to be trans, I find it very much harder to communicate the positive meanings.

I know that I am not just characterized by a history of suffering and misunderstanding; nor am I only a tightly-strung, highly electric nerve, sensitive to the least drift of molecules on the air, let alone to the ferocious terrors of prejudice and violence. I am also, as trans, something vital and meaningful and earthy: I must be. But I find this much harder to bring to awareness, let alone to speak. On the days when I'm not nursing, I work outdoors, gardening and building things—long hours as alone as possible, protected by earphones and the podcasts I listen to. I am lucky to live in a housing co-op, in Kitsilano, which consists of three old houses side by side, where the backyards are run together and so allow for big gardens, a few chickens, and a space for my tools and a chance to build things. It's a way to recover from the stresses of work, but it's also a kind of project to be trans in the light and air, amongst the small birds and the green leaves of the world, and to breathe myself into being through sawdust and capable hands and considered movement. If only there were a way to be trans in this way, too, in the larger, noisy world beyond my backyard.

So your email has occasioned another round of questioning about how to best be a nurse, and what it means—or should mean—as a trans person with sometimes trans patients. I am grateful to be reminded that I could be useful in this way.

I am also envious to hear of you building a cabin up north. I did construction work for a laneway housing company for a while, and still dream of building my own small house. If it weren't for coronavirus, I'd gladly invite you to come over and work together on something—there's endless work to do for the co-op, though most of it is less interesting than building a house—just for the sake of getting your hands on some tools and staying in practise before heading north again. It sounds as if you've already gotten a fair bit of experience, building concrete molds and so on, but hopefully the carpentry course will set you up for the next stages of your house.

Okay, so I think the two spaces after a period just looks better, no? I can never remember what's correct any more (about just about anything), but I care deeply about what looks good!

All the best,
Darach

15.

VOLCANO

Hi Ivan,

I just wanted to write and say thank you for sharing your stories out with the world.

There's a certain beauty in reading the words of "Shame: A Love Letter" at the end of *Rebent Sinner*, as this morning I woke up at 1 a.m. with anxiety in my chest and figured that was as good a time as any to start your book (and finish it apparently too)!

It was only a month ago that I got the chance to see you speak at the Nanaimo Public Library. That was also the same night I came out as trans to 2 of my friends and the first time I presented as feminine in public. I'd only been fitted for a wig 3 hours before, because I felt like if there was any moment in time where it'd be safe to take those first steps out the door in my transition, it'd be there. Didn't realize at the time that I'd be spending a quarter of the time trying to keep my newfound hair out of my face. Also didn't realize that being there would build me up to then go out and speak with my family and a few more friends about being trans over the following weeks.

It's still a long process of self-acceptance ahead of me, one that may never have an end, but one that I'm glad is finally moving. When I originally tried to come out, over 17 years ago now, there just weren't the positive role models out there in the public like there are now, so I allowed other people to define who I was and just spent a lot of years lost & confused. Your words give me courage and help me move forward.

That all being said, I have this vision of being in my late-70s and doing yoga on the top of a mountain in Hawaii at sunrise. That's my "gravy boat."

I hope that you're staying safe and healthy in the tough times of this pandemic. Looking forward to seeing you speak again the next time you're on the island.

All the best.

Sincerely,
Victoria Grey

Dear Victoria:

Thank you so much for sharing a little bit of your story with me. I first read your email on a Sunday morning, back in March, sitting in the easy chair in the corner of the living room, drinking coffee. And then ping—there it was.

I'm so grateful that you felt safe enough to spend some of your first hours presenting as feminine at my gig at the library that night. What an unknown honour it was for the rest of us, to be present with you and your friends, during such an important step forward. I hope you took pictures. I'm even more grateful that you took the time to write to me and tell me about it.

Some letters I can answer from my phone, in an airport, or waiting in line at the bank, or sitting in my car in a parking lot somewhere when I am ten minutes early for an appointment.

Other letters I need to think about. Ponder them while I am walking the dog first thing in the morning, with the mist still clinging to the edge of the day, or last thing at night, with the occasional waft of skunk insinuating itself into the dark from under the neighbours' dogwood hedge, or while pulling weeds in the front yard with the sun running sweat down the centre of my back, or peeling potatoes during the six o'clock news to make shepherd's pie for dinner. Doing something that leaves my hands just busy enough that my head is able to call the words in from the ether and start to put them into some kind of order.

Your letter was a need-to-think-about-it letter. I've read it many times now, first to locate its centre, and then to find the starting place for my reply.

I think I will begin with unpacking the word shame. I wrote that piece "Shame: A Love Letter" first as a Twitter thread, lying jet-lagged in a hotel bed in Malmo, Sweden, trying not to wake up my partner, Sarah. We had spent the day before on the beach with her family. They are all really nice people, let me state that unequivocally, before I say anything else, but I'm pretty certain I am the only trans person they really know, and there we were, all on the beach together. I remember sweating in the sturdy black tshirt I could not bring myself to take off that day, too scared to reveal my scars from my top surgery, and my insensate nipples, and my hard-won biceps, and my pasty not just Irish, but Canadian, and also Yukon skin, and thirty years of tattoos, in front of Sarah's mom and sister and brother-in-law and niece and nephew, all of whom look like they've just stepped out of a commercial for a Norwegian ski holiday, rosy-cheeked and wearing matching knit sweaters. Except they were in swimsuits that day, because it was August.

I want to make it clear that I sat there all day sweating in the sand because of my fears, not theirs.

The dictionary defines shame as "the feelings of being sad, embarrassed or guilty that you have when you know that something you have done is wrong or stupid."

So I guess, according to the Oxford dictionary, I misnamed that poem completely. I didn't feel sad or guilty, or even embarrassed that day. I didn't think I had done anything wrong, or stupid, either. I just felt like I didn't belong there, not that I wasn't welcome, just like I wasn't ready to unwrap the truth of me to them, not yet. Not beneath all that blue sky and under all that sun. What does the grey space between shame and fear smell like? Sweat, I would say.

Sometimes I just want to be judged by who I am, you know? Not what I am. I don't know if that makes any sense at all. I didn't want

Sarah's family, who I didn't know very well, to worry or wonder about what pronoun I use, or how to introduce me, or what my name used to be, and forget to find out that I am funny, and a good cook, and that I clean up after myself, and I adore their beloved Sarah just as much as they do. Until that day on the beach I guess I was just hoping that if I didn't draw attention to the situation, no one would notice that Sarah had brought home an ambiguously gendered storyteller from the Yukon named Ivan. I dunno. Sounds like a stretch, in retrospect.

I guess that road to self-acceptance that you wrote about in your letter is a long one, it turns out, and maybe parts of it are a bit of a traffic circle, if you know what I mean.

So by my math, you came out (this time) a little over six months ago. How is it all going? I suppose by now you have figured out which of the guys at work or school or yoga are the biggest transphobes, and hopefully someone has surprised you by being cooler and more supportive about it all than you thought they would be.

Hopefully you have tamed your wig and found some clothes that make you feel confident, and powerful. Unstoppable. Beautiful. I hope you are finding only love as you unwrap yourself.

Myself, I can't really remember an exact day, or moment, or even month or year that I finally came fully to terms with being and especially calling myself trans. I know that the I-am-the-only-one-on-this-crowded-beach feeling has been my shadow for all of my life. I've never been able to lose it, even at home under a high noon northern July sun and surrounded by those who know me the best, it still sticks to my heels and follows me everywhere.

I have come to the realization that, for me, part of being trans is just what the prefix itself means: *occurring in loanwords from Latin (transcend, transfix); on this model used with the meanings "across," "beyond," "through," "changing thoroughly," "transverse," in combination with elements of any origin: transempirical, transvalue. [Chemistry.]*

Trans was a word first and most commonly used in chemistry.

So basically I am a chemical poem that means beyond. I am moving and changing. I am borrowing an ancient word and altering it just enough to make my tongue recognize the shape of it in my own mouth.

I've never been to Hawaii but I intend to go for sure one day, sometime in The After of all of this. I've always dreamed of going there. I hope to meet you on top of that mountain on an island, with lava rolling red-orange and turning stone to liquid, and then cooling itself into another shape, deep under us both. There will be ash in the sky from the becoming. Our old bones will creak and snap at first, and we will stretch and breathe and move as the sun comes up and shows us another day, made new.

With so much love,
Ivan

16.

TEETER-TOTTER

MARCH 29, 2020

Hi Ivan,

It feels equal parts like your show at Nanaimo north library was last week and also in a whole other time. How odd the world and time we live in now. You recognized my name when I came up to get my copy of *Rebent Sinner* signed and told me to send you a letter. I will admit, part of the reason this is so late is because I've been trying to figure out if you have a P.O. box or something like that to send handwritten letters to. You seem like the person who would appreciate that, reading through them between work on your sauna and any other project up there in the north.

I'm writing this as I listen to yours' and Sarah's livestream show on Facebook, and I'm finding myself so incredibly thankful for technology in this current world. We're all searching for words, for ways to comprehend this global shift going on. And I am thankful that technology gave you both the opportunity to share words to us and for me to be able to collect words from you two.

This is technically the fourth show I've seen of yours. In each one, you tell the Pulse story, of calling up your dad. And that story in particular always punches. Not just because I was a month fresh out of the closet as a trans guy when the Pulse shooting happened, and I remember sitting in downtown Calgary with dozens of others as we mourned and got angry, but specifically because of the conversation with your dad. And how, in the story, you talk about how you almost didn't call him, because you were so angry with him.

I've been angry at my dad for a long time. Just about everyone looked at me and went "yeah, we know" when I came out as trans. Glass closet,

I was in. But he said such horrible things, over and over again since I've come out, shit you really shouldn't say to your kid. He's called me things no father should call his kids, we've gotten into some major fights (loud enough that neighbours asked if they needed to call the cops), and there is a harsh distance between us now that I am gone and in Nanaimo. I want to be a better man, and that probably means forgiving him, letting myself understand all the pain and trauma he's also trying to work through which probably fuels his reaction to me. But my dysphoria has his voice now, and it's going to take a lot of work to separate that. Every time I come across that story of yours, it makes me sit with this all and suss out a bit more of the tangled mess. And maybe one of these days I'll phone him to see how he's doing.

This is already feeling like a long piece, I hope that's okay. I think about the Nanaimo library show a lot. I felt so seen that night. Every story you shared seemed to connect with something in my life, and it felt like you were creating a space that was 100% for us queer trans peeps. I felt safe, all wrapped up there in your stories. That night did so much for my soul, and I appreciate what you do to make sure we have words, we know we're not alone.

Say hi to Sarah and Lucky for me. All of you; stay safe, stay healthy. And thank you,

— Lys

Dear Lys:

Oh, my friend. Let me begin this letter by saying that I am so sorry that your father has treated you so cruelly since you came out to him. I know that these words have probably been spoken to you already by many of your friends and loved ones, but please let me add my voice to theirs, and say that nobody, at any age, should ever have to hear stuff like that coming out of the mouth of their parent.

It's been almost seven months since that show at the library in Nanaimo. I got so many emails and messages in the days and weeks after that gig, I'm just now getting to answering all of them. I got way more mail than I usually do from a show with an audience of that size (I'd estimate it was about 200 people there?) and I have spent quite a bit of time thinking about why that might be. It was my last fully public show before the pandemic hit, so maybe it was the last event many of the people there that night went to see? Maybe we all had more time on our hands in those first strange weeks of lockdown? Maybe we were all responding to our sudden need for connection, for contact, for correspondence? I'm still not sure.

Your email was one of the hardest for me to know how to respond to. How not to sound trite? What if I say the wrong thing, to someone who is hurting, and who shared some of that hurt with me? How to stay in my lane, as I am a storyteller, with no training or credentials as a counsellor or therapist? I so don't want to even suggest that you put your heart in danger's path by contacting your father, just because I do that on the regular, and to my detriment at times, to be certain. So, I will just answer you as a storyteller—with my chest cracked open and my ears turned all the way up, and holding hope for you in one hand, and the other stretched out to help you up the hill behind me.

I just last night told my partner Sarah that my father has broken my heart more times and more deeply than all the other heartaches this life has brought to me, combined. Some of those cracks in this heart of mine I can blame on his battles with alcohol, and depression, some I can follow home to his own trauma, his own pain, but some I just cannot. It hurts just to type the truth here that my father has also harmed me, and people I love, with his own selfishness and narcissism and lack of ability to truly listen to, or care about, others. Even still, as I write these words, I worry about hurting his feelings, were he to ever read them. Like I am somehow betraying him with the truth of us.

Let me tell you a story. About 15 years ago I called my dad up on the phone. He almost never calls me, maybe a handful of times in my entire life, and most of the times he has called me, he has been drunk. One time he wanted guitar lessons. Another time he was with a woman on a date, and wanted to ask for advice about how to go about publishing her poetry, another time he was on another date with a different woman, and wanted to know where I had stashed the keys to my travel trailer that I had stored in his backyard, because she wanted to see the inside of it. Anyway.

About 15 years ago I called him up on the phone. It's always hard to know right away if he has been drinking, even if he's quite drunk, he's just that good at it, and he will lie if you simply ask him outright.

There are clues, I have learned over the years. The sound of ice cubes tinkling in his glass used to be one, before he went to rehab and kicked the scotch habit and switched to red wine. He smokes more when he drinks, so the sound of a lighter striking and that first long inhale can be another.

I could hear the TV on in the background, and his wife Pat was still alive, puttering in the tiny kitchen off of the main room in their little house. It was before she got sick that first time.

I forget what I was telling him, but I remember him interrupting me and blurting out, "You know something I've always wondered about? Why is it that you guys have to have a gay pride parade? Why can't you just be who you are, what's with the leather and the feathers and the glitter? Why do you need to make such a big deal about it? It's your own business what you do. It's private. The rest of us don't need to have a parade to announce we're normal. What is it with gay people that you need to march around and yell it at everyone else?"

I think I stumbled part way through saying something about how straight people had all kinds of parades, parades for football teams and beauty pageants and Santa Claus and Canada Day, and the fact that he had such a problem with queer people gathering to celebrate and dress up and fight for our freedom and human rights was a sign that we still really needed to gather and march, and I think that is right about when things took a nasty turn. Sounds like I don't need to tell you some of the things he said to me that day. I don't remember for sure who hung up on who, but I think it was me.

Six or seven months passed. At first I was just angry. Righteous. Then the guilt started to seep in a little. He was a small-town guy, I figured. Probably caught a clip of an ass peeking out between black leather chaps, or a nipple ring, or rainbow-painted big old bulldyke boobs on the six o'clock television news, and it freaked him out. He came to me for an explanation and I got defensive, I started to argue with myself. I had allowed that defensiveness to shut down an opportunity to educate him, and that was on me. It was my fault, at least part of it was, and I needed to talk to him and work it out.

I avoided calling him for a couple more weeks, maybe another month. Finally, on a quiet Sunday afternoon when I had had a couple of days off from the road, and the laundry was done, and the chicken was roasting in the oven, and the rain was falling outside, I called him up.

"Hey," I said. "I know it's been months since we talked."

"Has it?" he said, clearing his throat and lighting a smoke.

I took a deep breath. "I wanted to apologize for my part in the fight we had that last time we talked."

"We had a fight?" He asks. "About what?"

"About Gay Pride, remember? You said you didn't understand why gay people even had parades, and I got defensive and we got into a scrap about it, and I think I hung up on you."

"Well I don't blame you," he said. "Sounds like I was being an asshole."

And then he changed the subject.

Seven months. Seven months, maybe more, I packed around feelings about that fight, shifting them from one shoulder to the other shoulder, and he was blissfully unencumbered. He didn't even remember it the morning after it first happened.

All this to say, I understand if you choose not to pick up that phone, I really do.

I guess for me it's a bit of a teeter-totter, rocking back and forth between duty and damage, hope for change, and disappointment. He lives alone, 200 kilometres away from his brothers or other family. I worry too much when I don't speak to him. My sister is disabled, and they have an even more fraught relationship than he and I do, and she is more susceptible to his careless and tiny cruelties than I am. If I don't step up to look after him, I fear that my mother will, even though they divorced 25 years ago, and she shouldn't have to.

And try as I might, even though some days I am quite sure it would be better for me if I could, I just cannot let go of this dream that he will sober up. I can't stop wishing that after a few days his hands will stop shaking enough that he can get up off of the couch and clean up his shop, and finish replacing the seals in the engine of his boat, and get it back out on the water, and let the last of this summer's sun make him squint and smile and warm his old bones just enough that maybe he feels like dropping a line in our spot where the little river joins the lake, just to see if anything is biting.

So I'm not going to give you any advice about how to deal with your dad, because I cannot even follow my own.

But I want you to know that I hear you, I do, and I see you. You are not alone. In fact, I think we could fill a ferry boat, one of those giant new ones that sail to Nanaimo from Horseshoe Bay on Labour Day weekend, with trans people of all stripes—trans people who don't talk at all, or who don't talk enough, or about the right things, with our fathers, and we could sail together to an island somewhere, and take each other fishing. Stay up late sitting on the beach around the fire, telling stories. And listening to each other.

Yeah. That would be sweet.

Please keep in touch Lys.

With love and compassion,
Ivan

P.S. I'm going to get a P.O. box. Good idea. I will send you the address as soon as I have it. I truly do love a good letter.

17.

GABARDINE PANTS

DECEMBER 16, 2017

Hey Coyote,

My name is Kate—I'm a 25-year-old bookseller who lives on Vancouver Island. I grew up in Halifax.

My story is not unique, and then is, as everyone's personal stories are. I grew up inexplicably angry in dresses. Too rough to play with the girls, but too sensitive to hang only with the boys (I also read a lot, and bored easily). Painfully rejected by my older sister because I wanted to snowboard. I loved the mud and rain. I wanted to build things.

Kicked out of elementary social circles for not wanting to play house. Grew a little older and never thought twice about dressing to fit in. I went to an inner-city school—where the white-bread middle-class kids were mixed with the kids of absentee fathers. Ditched, locked away, alcoholic. Kids who were first-gen Canadians, pushed and taunted for their differences. Kids who were raising themselves. Siblings who stuck together to create a small island of refuge. Kids who knew, saw, understood much more than they should have at ages 7, 8, 9. The sexual world came into my understanding at age 6. We learned about death in the 2nd grade, when one of our 6th-grade students committed suicide. There was no way I was going to risk being my True Self. I became a more private child. I still wore my brother's hand-me-downs, my older (male) cousin's, all summer. During the school year I wore what all the other girls wore. I chose wisely. I had a keen eye and was born an observer. I knew exactly how to fit in.

What I didn't realize, however, was the little warrior I was shutting away in a very small, very soundproof box. She had short black hair, like her brother, and was an expert tree climber. As time passed and life in the Maritimes moved into the late 90s, That little warrior grew tired of screaming inside her master's soundproof box. He got so tired, he lay down to sleep.

My childhood friend comes out to me at 12. Something deep inside me leaps to the ceiling of my stomach, trying to climb up my throat. I swallow it. I hug her, but we don't talk about it. We continue as friends, no questions asked. She has a bravery I lack.

Teenage years:
I trained as a competitive gymnast. I hear my peers joking about how the simple fact of all-boy-exposure of one of our male coaches "made him gay."

I had never questioned the deep safety I felt around my coach. We had some weird unspoken bond, where I felt like I could lay my head on his shoulder when I needed to. He was 6 years older than me. I never wondered what it was, just grateful to have the bubble we did.

High School:
I become friends with Martin, a boy I know is homo. This makes me trust him. It also makes me hate myself, but I don't understand why.

I grow. My hips are in the wrong spot. Too high up, like someone stretched them when I wasn't looking. I yearn for my childlike body again, where boys' and girls' hips are in the same place.

Age 20:
I ask my best friend if she had ever thought about us as anything more than friends. She is obviously repulsed. I say nothing. We never speak of it again.

I discover tumblr. The internet's goldmine of LGBTQ truth. (This is 2011, mind you. Tumblr has not quite blown up with millennials quite yet. It is our MySpace). I discover girlsex makes me excited. Like really, really excited. It is my little secret. Tumblr is my private world. There are others like me. But I'm not one of them, am I? I like boys. I like attention from boys. I like feeling strong arms around me. I educate myself on Roman relationships. It was natural for younger women to have an older woman "guide her" in the natures of sexual exploration. It helped prepare them for marriage. I am normal, I am normal.

Age 23:
I am in art school. I am hopelessly in love with a girl in my film class. She is Out—everyone is—it's art school for fuck's sake. I realize I am Deeply Uncomfortable with myself. I also can't really speak around her.

We hook up one night in the film department, after hours. It is mind-blowing. My entire universe has just doubled.

I am set to move away 2 weeks from that night. I panic. I leave without giving her the goodbye, or explanation she deserves. It's a phase. Shame haunts my every waking minute. I am not normal, not normal.

Age 25:
I have just ended the perfect relationship with the perfect man. His only goal is to support me in my endeavours. His mother gives me the maternal love I missed out on as a child (insert classic working-mom-docs-all, Mum is too tired to give 3rd child attention, 3rd child requires "too much love"). His sister is lovely. It is not enough. I am missing something, left wanting.

I cannot get my best girl friend out of my head. She is queer and comfortable. She looks at me in a way that makes me feel naked, exposed. We hooked up once the previous summer. We were on drugs. It was just fun. Somewhere inside me, my little warrior wakes up. He is banging on the glass. I push away. She gives me space, but comes back around. She has been nothing but supportive of my current hetero relationship.

I cannot get her out of my head.

I end the relationship.

I am not heartbroken, but he is.

Same story, different man. I feel like a monster.

I watch hetero couples in my town. I am envious. I want to want that.

I want to be like everyone else.

*   *   *   *

Your teen book, *One in Every Crowd*, stares at me from the shelf at work.

I take it down, but don't read it. Oh no, I can't bear to open it. I can feel it holds truths I am not ready to know.

It sits next to me at work for 6 hours. I pick it up, put it down.

Finally I force myself to open it. Fall off the deep end. Fall into trust.

Thank for you affirming every confusing experience in my life.

Thank you for giving me courage.

Thank you for making me feel loved.

Thank you for showing me how to love myself.

Thank you for being me, at age 6, with that bicycle and the twins-kissing-plan and the I-don't-know tears. I have been that child.

Thank you for changing my life.

. . . Sorry about the novel. I know you're busy.

With love and affection and explosive rainbows and velvet pirate pants and Lou Reed lyrics,
Kate

Dear Kate:

Wow. What a letter. Where to start?

My first question is obvious, really—just what Lou Reed lyrics are you referring to? Did you know that "Perfect Day" was on the B-side of the 45 of "Walk on the Wild Side?" Am I too old for the significance of that to even translate for you?

You were 25 back in 2017. So you're 28 now? I just checked my email to be sure. I wrote you back a short note three days later, three years ago. I thanked you for your beautiful letter (I meant it), and told you I would file it away in my rainy day folder and read it again when I needed to. And that is exactly what I did.

It's the first week of September now. The beginning of what looks to be the second wave of the pandemic has closed bars and restaurants again in British Columbia, but school started this week somehow, all across the country. I am in Ontario. It's raining outside my bedroom window. I'm 51 years old and I've just read your letter again three times. I must have really needed it. You are a great writer.

It sounds to me like if I had been born 27 years later, and/or if you had grown up in the Yukon instead of Nova Scotia, we might have met on the first day of grade two and bonded over our shared love of brown corduroy pants or Harriet the Spy or our matching dark-blue bikes.

I hear echoes of my own experience in some of your story, and in other ways we were very different. I wasn't too rough to play with the girls, I just spoke a different language, and practised a different religion than they did. I worshipped tree forts and my Meccano set and art supplies and books about dogs and bugs and grand adventures. Most girls I knew or read about in books didn't seem to want to go on grand adventures, which was why I loved Pippi and Harriet and Nancy Drew and Jo from *The Facts of Life* so much.

The thought of wearing a dress to school gave me cold-throated nightmares in the dark, and what we would now call panic attacks come morning, but back in 1974 it was just called being difficult and getting on everyone's last nerve for no good reason.

By grade one my mother and I had come to a tentative peace regarding my wardrobe, I was not forced to wear a dress to school anymore, but I now had three pairs of gabardine dress pants hanging ominously in my closet. My mom's friend Linda sewed them for me by hand from a pattern she got at Woolworth's. I tried to like them, but I just couldn't. No belt loops. No pockets. I conveniently forgot those slacks (my grandmother's word for them) existed, and I wore jeans or corduroys to school, except for picture day and Valentine's Day, because I didn't want to get Valentine's cards only from the girls in my class who had been trained since birth to be nice and make a card for everyone, even me and Danny C. with his crocheted bookbag, and the new kid who peed his pants in dodgeball that one time. I didn't want a boyfriend, but this was a secret I told absolutely no one, not even myself. I didn't want to be a boy, either, but I was already very familiar with failing at being a girl, and I was completely unaware of any other options.

I just called my mom to ask her what was the name of her friend the seamstress, and she told me to remember that back in 1974 there was a lot of pressure to dress your kid a certain way, to conform, to not stick out or else there would be judgement and questions especially if you were a very young mother who didn't have any money back then, with a schoolboy-faced husband who worked out in the bush and was never around for parent-teacher interviews and such, and I believe her. She tells me her great-niece, my second cousin, went to her first day of school today wearing tights, a dress over that, a jacket over that all in mismatched colours, odd long socks and a hat with ears on it. No one batted an eye, she tells me. Things are different now.

The news today is full of that story about the forest fire in California that was started by errant fireworks at a gender reveal party and has now destroyed over 10,000 acres and rendered many homeless.

All I can think of is that poor fetus, and how much I hope they don't grow up to hate their clothes as much as we did, no matter what sex they are assigned at birth, and whatever gender they end up being.

When I was six or seven I signed up for boys' hockey. I was the only girl in the league and I had to change into my equipment alone in a mop closet, next to a stinking galvanized rolling bucket and a shelf full of bleach bottles. The janitor at the Jim Light Arena had decided I had spunk and cleared out a corner for me in his supply room, and built me a solo bench, hung up a hook above that for my parka and, best of all, stuck up a picture of number 99 Wayne Gretzky on the wall opposite my bench, with my school photo taped over Wayne's face.

I met my first ever gay man in grade eight. My saxophone ensemble was hired to play intermission at the Guild Hall theatre and Arthur Giovinnazzo was sweating behind the bar, both of his wrists jingling with six inches of silver bangles and a diamond earring glinting in his right ear, which everyone knew was the gay ear. He was dancing unabashed and alone to "Tainted Love" by Soft Cell while expertly pouring glasses of wine and winking at almost everyone. I was thirteen years old and I could not stop watching him but could not meet his gaze or speak a single word to him. Three years later he hired me as a waitress at his restaurant the No Pop Sandwich Shop.

He fired me unceremoniously and effective immediately a couple of months later, on my sixteenth birthday, for taking too long to give menus to a new table because I was distracted by another giant table full of my friends who were not ordering enough and eating too slow. He told me I was the worst waitress the world had ever seen. I don't remember this next bit, but Arthur swears I packed up my backpack and on my way out the door I turned and told him that he wasn't being fair. That the world was a really big place and that statistically there had to be someone in it who was a worse waitress than I was.

We are still friends, to this day.

I think it was that same summer I first saw the lesbian letter carrier from afar. I had another part-time job at a little art gallery downtown, and she delivered the mail there. She didn't even come in, or look up, or notice me at all, she would just drop the letters in the brass mailbox nailed to the post outside the front door, but I couldn't swallow for about twenty minutes after she disappeared around the corner at the end of the block. Her salt-and-pepper hair was shorn close to the sides of her head and the muscles in her calves haunted me whenever I thought about them, which I endeavoured never to do.

I don't know what my young life would have been like if I had read a queer book or seen a movie with a gay character in it. I do remember Billy Crystal playing a gay man on some sitcom my aunties watched in the early seventies, but he was the butt of all jokes, the lisping target of derisive laugh tracks. There was John Ritter's character Jack Tripper pretending he was gay (which mostly consisted of fluttering his eyelashes and drooping at the wrist) on *Three's Company* so that Mr. Roper would let him live platonically with Janet and Chrissy. Neither of these characters revealed anything to me about being gay, other than it was something I most definitely did not want to be.

The first trans character I remember seeing in a movie was Dil in *The Crying Game*. Even the man who loved her vomited the first time she took her clothes off in front of him.

That movie came out in 1992. I was twenty-three years old. I'm pretty sure this is a coincidence, but that is right around the time I really started to get serious about my writing.

I never set out to be a queer author. I really didn't. I just loved writing and especially telling stories. I know now in retrospect that I was feeding and watering a vast and hollow space inside of myself—an old mirror in a haunted house that did not reflect anything when I looked into it.

I'm so glad that you found my stories when you needed them, Kate, I really am.

I sincerely think you should keep writing. I really do. Right now somewhere there is someone being born who one day is going to need to pull a borrowed book off of a shelf and read your story. They will see themselves in those pages, and take courage in your words.

Maybe one day they will take the time to write you a long letter, and you will read it, and you will know that you made the right decision, sitting down like you did and putting all of those words down onto that empty white screen. Filling that mirror for all of those future kind-of-like-yous who so needed to see themselves, who needed to know that someone who resembles them lived, and was loved, and is remembered.

Your friend,
Ivan

18.

ON CAMERA

Hi there Ivan. I don't often do this, but occasionally I find myself writing to people who've helped me through particularly tough times. You're one such person. My girlfriend introduced me to you and your poetry last year. Through your voice, for the first time, I came closest to recognising my core self.

I'm an actress from Pakistan, female, gay. I grew up in a world absent of any vocabulary which wasn't hetero-normative. In college I finally came to terms with my gay self, but I still felt a sense of shame at being "butch," or feeling masculine in a very feminist environment. I eventually became a professional actress and being a public figure in a Muslim country is not very conducive to letting one's true self shine through, especially if you're gay. The pain of having to wear makeup and feminine clothes on stage, on TV, in front of thousands of people has been almost a physical one. I remember the first time my mother tried to put makeup on me, I let her do it but unbidden tears were streaming down my face the whole time. Discovering you and other courageous butch women online has given me strength to break free of a world to which I've always wanted to belong. I've moved to London to regain some sanity, and am going to try and get my partner to join me eventually. And if all goes well, I can live a true and honest life without any more lies and guilt.

Late night emails are never a good idea, but I've been meaning to get in touch with you for a few months now, and it being pride week and all, I thought I'd finally get to it. So thank you :)

Warm regards
Ayesha

P.S. I'm still closeted in Pakistan, because coming out will create a lot of trouble for my family, so I'd like to request you to keep this to yourself if possible. And I do see the irony :)

JULY 7, 2013

Dear Ayesha:

Thank you for your beautiful and heartfelt letter.

I am just recovering from a pretty major surgery that I had about a month ago, so I am just now trying to catch up on the pile of emails that came in while I was on the mend. I really appreciate hearing from you, and reading your story, so I wanted to just drop you a line and let you know that.

Good luck settling back down in London, and I wish you strength and love and patience on your journey to yourself.

sincerely,
Ivan

Hey Ivan. Thank you for writing back. Your email really made my day. And sorry to hear about your surgery. I hope all is well now, and also that you get back to 110% very soon. You have the good will and prayers of many many women across the world (and maybe some men too).

Warm regards
Ayesha

P.S. Sending you a poem I wrote, along with prayers and positive vibes. I originally wrote this in Urdu, based on the concept of who we are when we're naked, without clothes to aid in constructing identity. Hope you like it :)

Dear Ayesha:

A little over seven years has passed since our last email, and I find myself wondering how you are doing. Before the pandemic, I would probably have just continued to wonder. Now, it's nearly midnight on a Thursday in September, and I am sitting down to write you and simply ask you how you are. Are you still in London? Are you still acting? How is your artist's heart weathering this pandemic? I send you my love wherever you are, and my hopes that you and your family are safe and healthy.

My partner Sarah is a musician, and most of her family is in Sweden and Norway. It has been a long, hard summer for her. Not only has she had to cancel all her tours and gigs, she is unable to travel home and has had to do all the things daughters and sisters do over WhatsApp and FaceTime: worry about her mom, laugh and argue with her sister, watch her niece and nephew start grade one and speak a full sentence for the first time. I have not seen my family in the Yukon since the pandemic began, either, but at least I know that I could get on a plane or get in a car and drive to see them if there was an emergency, and just knowing that is possible has made it easier for me than it is for her, separated from her blood by an ocean of salt water.

Just as you have probably done over the last months, we have spent many hours wondering what the entertainment industry is going to look like for the next few years. She is downstairs in her studio now, working on her new album, and I am at my desk, writing. Both of us doing the only things we have ever known how to do to help sort through and make sense of the swirl and pitch inside of our chests and heads. I write stories and she writes songs.

I just read the poem you sent me, again. Thank you for sharing it with me. I wish I could read it in its original Urdu, but I read it out loud and thought about who we are naked, without clothes to aid in constructing identity.

There is a mirror next to my desk, which is in the bedroom where I sleep. Every morning when I get out of bed I walk past that mirror. Some days naked, some days wearing only boxer shorts, which are kind of an identity statement on their own, now that your song makes me think about it.

I like my body more in the mornings than I do at night, for some reason.

Do you remember in our emails way back, when I wrote that I was recovering from a surgery? On June 3, 2013 I had a radical double mastectomy. Top surgery. After decades of struggling to feel right in this body of mine, I had my breasts removed. Next to quitting smoking cigarettes back in 2008, having top surgery was the single best thing I ever did for my health in my life.

I passed my seven-year anniversary of that surgery this summer, and I did what I am now able to do every morning: get up, put on a tshirt, and go downstairs to make coffee. No bra, no binder. Just my shirt slipping over my skin. I am as happy in my body now as I have ever been since I was ten years old or so, back before I realized that I was not pretty, and that pretty mattered more than just about anything else a girl could be. I have moments now, mostly while in the water, where I forget to hate anything about this body I am in.

I just read your letters again. And then again. I found myself tearing up when I read your words about growing up in a world absent of any words that were not hetero-normative. About feeling masculine in a feminist environment. About the nearly physical pain you experienced having to wear make-up and feminine clothing on stage in front of thousands of people.

I'm not sure how old you are, but I am imagining tiny butch you in Pakistan, and tiny butch me on the other side of the world in the Yukon, you confusing your Muslim mother and me confounding my Catholic one. What comfort we could have brought each other, were I even to have spotted you, trailing along behind your mother and aunt and cousins on the street somewhere. I like to think we would have still recognized each other, even in our straight girl costumes.

I know that being out of the closet is a privilege, and it is one that I do not take for granted. Thank you for reminding me that being able to be visibly butch or non-binary in this world is also a privilege of a sort, too. It is easy to forget this when I am being screeched at in a women's bathroom, or with my heart pounding in the last stall in a men's bathroom in an airport on the road somewhere. There are so many kinds of bravery, and not all of them are as easy to spot in a crowd as being a butch is.

I wish we had more words. I wish there was another word for not-feminine than just the word masculine. I've never felt called to the word androgynous, I see this word as meaning ambiguous, and you and I both know that there is nothing ambiguous about being a masculine person in a body the world doesn't expect this of. I wish there was no line in the sand between the word butch and the words non-binary or trans. I look in that mirror every morning and see something that fits none of these words and all of them simultaneously. But even still, I know that you are my sister.

My younger sister is named Caroline. We call her Carrie for short. Several years ago she was working in a hardware store, in the paint department, alongside a guy named Carl, that I went to school with.

Carl is one of a couple of boys I grew up with who came out of the closet after we all graduated. No one came out in high school in the Yukon back then, it just wasn't safe. Anyway.

Carl and Carrie were chatting away at work one day when it was slow in the store, and she mentioned her sister. Carl got very terse with Carrie, and explained to her that I was trans, didn't she know, and that she couldn't call me her sister anymore, that I was her brother now and she needed to get it together and be respectful of my gender identity.

Carrie took her coffee break and escaped to sit in her truck in the parking lot to have a cigarette. She called me in tears. What am I supposed to call you now? She sobbed. You've only ever been my sister. You never told me to call you anything else.

I told her that I never asked her to call me anything but her sister because I will never be anything but her sister. I told her that she and I get to decide what we call each other, not Carl, not the world, not anyone.

So. Ayesha, my butch sister. I hope you get up in the morning and greet your naked self with nothing but love, and know that no matter what clothes you wear out the door and in front of that camera, that I can see exactly who you are, and I know that the truth of us both is found in the spaces between words and labels, not inside of the words themselves.

This is why labels peel off in the water.

I am sending you a song that my partner Sarah wrote for her best friend in Sweden, a song meant to travel across the ocean, until Sarah is able to make the trip herself.

I remain your sister,
Ivan

19.

GENTLE MELT

Hey,

I'm Connor, an Aussie 18-year-old and I just wanted to thank you. I came out to my parents as trans about three years ago, since then the most acceptance I've gotten is a couple of drunken conversations with my mum that either she forgets the next day or chooses to ignore and the purchasing of a binder for my birthday when I finally managed to prove to her just how badly I needed one. My dad has remained silent and I don't know if that'll ever change.

The extended portion of my family are half the world away and I haven't seen them since I was barely old enough to toddle, so a support system from them doesn't really exist. I've got a brother who doesn't know and a sister who does but lives six hours away. I'm not able to move out and since I've just left school I'm finally able to start being myself.

My mum's never really understood, stuck in that phase where you voice your acceptance but don't act on it. But I went on holidays for a week and when I came back she was acting different, singing praises about your book *Tomboy Survival Guide*. I thought it was weird how excited she was, going on about how it had changed her perspective and urging me to read it. I wasn't expecting much, not with that title, half dreading that it was gonna be some bullshit about some trans man who'd realised he wasn't a man, just a tomboy or a butch or whatever. But I got why she loved it so much soon enough.

It's different and it's new and it's (for lack of a better word) nitty-gritty, giving an insight into the trans perspective that you don't really find anywhere else. My mum was especially touched by the mention of your name change and its connection to family, something that's been a huge contention between us. I guess I was lucky in the same way you were, my sister was named for my dad and my brother for my mum, whilst my name has no such connection.

She's started to think about things differently, not completely there yet, but closer than she was and your book, coupled with a video from a LGBT friend's wedding where she said that I looked the happiest I had in a long time (wearing a suit and going by my own name). We're waiting for *Gender Failure* to come into our library and I'm currently trying to hunt down a copy of *Close to Spider Man*, but I can't find one anywhere locally.

So I know this is disjointed and jumps around a bit (I'm more of an artist than a writer), but I wanted to thank you, not because you performed some miracle and completely changed my mum's mind, but because you planted that notion for change.

I've been through hell the last couple of years, therapy, depression, anxiety, self-harm, but I'm finally in a place where I feel relatively safe and comfortable and a portion of that is due to you. I'm looking into HRT at the moment and about to start the process of legally changing my name, I was always going to do both these things and that was never gonna go any differently. But you've helped to give me that little bit of hope that when I come out the other side feeling a little bit more like me, that I'll have my mum by my side.

Thank you,
Connor.

Dear Connor:

I know I wrote you back a couple of days after I first received your email back in 2017, but it was just a short note, and your letter deserved so much better a response than I was able to give you back then, so here I am, writing you the letter I wish I had sent you three years ago.

It is six months pretty much to the day since we "sheltered at home" in the first days of the pandemic. Most of my family still lives in the Yukon, where I was born and raised, and due to travel restrictions and quarantine rules, and my new job here in Ontario, I have not seen my northern family since before the pandemic began, and I truly do not know when I will be able to go home again. This has reframed my feelings about my giant family quite a bit, and I find myself missing them in whole new ways, even the messy and complicated facets of coming from a big family that I never imagined myself longing for, or feeling the lack of.

I miss my mom the most, I think. She had to pack up her place and move this summer. She just turned 71 last month, and it was hard to not be able to come home and help her with everything. I've only seen her new condo when my sister FaceTimed once with me and walked her cell phone around from room to room for a virtual tour. I caught flashes of my mom in the background, waving and pointing to her new gas fireplace and showing me the insides of the kitchen cupboards. Her hair is all gone silver now, and she looked smaller than she seemed last winter, somehow.

She was the first person in my family that I came out to as queer, back when I was eighteen, also. It didn't go very well. She was pro-gay rights in word, and at her work, where she helped to draft a benefits package that included same-sex partners for Yukon territorial government workers, in 1984, one of the first of its kind anywhere in Canada. She had lesbian friends and made every effort to show her support of them and be their ally. But with me, she was silent and distant about it all. She never brought any of it up and quickly squelched any conversation about my girlfriends, or my life. She seemed overly cool and uncomfortable around any of my gay friends. I felt like she was ashamed of who I was, and for many years I practiced matching her silence with my own.

I don't remember the exact moment when it all began to change. I imagine it now like watching a frozen lake begin to thaw, at first you begin to hear a faint and distant trickle, beneath what remains of the previous winter's collected snowfalls under all that hard and blue ice. Then one afternoon after a couple of days of sun that trickle becomes a stream, and the ice becomes increasingly fragile, and the snow melts and contributes to the now-insistent rush of water which starts to break bits of the ice off and the next thing you know it's April in the Yukon and the swans are back and the willow bushes are flashing their soft and furry buds and promising silver-green leaves and it's finally safe to leave your parka at home.

Maybe none of that last paragraph makes any sense at all to an Australian, now that I read it back to myself.

What I'm trying to say is how glad I am that I didn't stay frozen on the wrong end of what I once felt was my mother's shame about who I was.

It took me decades to realize that homophobia was the wrong word for what I saw in my mom's face and heard in her voice those first few years. She wasn't as afraid of the queer in me, as she was afraid for her queer baby in the world and in the place she lived in. Inside of the only family she knew. She was terrified of what the world was going to do to her oldest child. It was 1987 and all of her fears were justifiable. Some days I even wonder if her subconscious knew I was trans before I even did, and if that contributed to her wishing I was less visible, less obvious. If she wanted to close those closet doors to keep me safe, not silenced.

My dad was another story, and still is. I can't tell where his inability to understand who I am ends, and his lack of interest in anyone's life outside of his own begins. The booze doesn't help clarify any of it, and I know from your letter that you understand what I mean by that. My father taught me how to drive a stick shift, how to catch a fish, how to drive a forklift, how to weld, how to make a perfect pancake, and the difference between a Robertson, Phillips and flathead screw, but the biggest lesson I learned from him is how practicing and modelling the wrong kind of masculinity gets in the way of so much that should live in the space between us. So much love and tenderness and compassion and forgiveness and nurturing, not just between our fathers and ourselves, but between our fathers and themselves, too. I'm working on learning to forgive him so that one day I can help him to forgive himself. To accept the help and love he needs more than ever. To have mercy upon himself. I'm starting to see that his survival depends on this.

I spent last Christmas in London, Ontario, with my partner Sarah. Her dad's partner, Lorie, invited Sarah and I over to her sister's place for a Sunday afternoon Christmas party. Lorie's family is even bigger and louder and rougher around the edges than mine is, which is saying a lot, and I felt immediately comfortable around this unruly mob of blue-collar medium-sized town people. Nobody cooked anything, the kitchen table was full of veggie plates from Costco and bowls containing six different kinds of chips and a bucket of KFC and a frozen and thawing strawberry cheesecake.

Someone's dog peed on the carpet when someone's uncle stepped on its foot and two nearly identical but not twin brothers teased each other about their receding hairlines and growing bellies. One of Lorie's nephews shrugged his brand-new Christmas button-down shirt off of his shoulders to show off the new tattoo on his back. I felt about as at home as I ever have at somebody else's family's Christmas party.

There was a young kid slouched on the couch in the living room, staring at their phone, not talking much to anyone. Lorie introduced him to me, and I could tell by the way she said his name slowly, Ang-us, in two syllables, that I should for some reason pay attention. That is when I noticed the silhouette of a binder lurking underneath his black tshirt. The shy sloop of his shoulders. He did not look up from under his long eyelashes at me. Kept staring at his phone.

Why don't you ask Ivan if they will sign your book for you? Lorie's sister asked. Angus shrugged and slid off the couch and lumbered over to the Christmas tree and retrieved a shiny and unopened copy of my book *Tomboy Survival Guide* and passed it to me.

All this to say, I don't think you were the only trans kid out there who wasn't immediately excited that I called that book what I did. My only defense is, *Non-Binary Human Who Also Identifies as Trans but Who Still Resonates With the Word Butch But Knows Not Everybody Does, and Who Grew Up Thinking the Only Word That Sort of Fit Her (Later Them), Was Tomboy, Survival Guide* is way too long of a title, even for me.

I'm so glad that my book found its way into your hands, and grateful that you were able to overlook the title and open it and find some comfort and familiarity in its pages. When I have hard writing days I think about the slow melt between you and your mom, and I sit down and open my laptop and make myself put one word in front of the other, drip by drip, and continue.

Please send me your address and I will sign a copy of my book that came out last fall, and put it in the mail for you.

I hope this letter finds you well, and twenty-one years old now, and a little bit more you every day. I hope your mom is right by your side, smiling and proud, and unafraid.

Please keep in touch.

Your friend,
Ivan

20.

KEEP TENDER

Dear Ivan,

I just finished *Rebent Sinner*. Every time I read a book that resonates with my soul I feel poetic. And so, seeing all your appreciation for letters, I'm sending you one.

The first time I read *Stone Butch Blues* I cried and immediately read it four more times. I'd seen the word butch before, but not like that. My family was military, so I didn't have elders I knew. I hardly had queers I knew. The moving kept me from knowing more than my own peers. I regret that. I don't know if you like being called an elder. Every trans person your age who mentions the word elder seems to have a bit of melancholy in their breath. I suppose, given a few decades, I'll find out.

I used to live in Alaska. The first time I saw the Yukon, it stole my breath. I've been all over North America and I still say it's the most beautiful place I've been. When I was in Alaska I knew weirdos like myself. I was 10. I'm the only queer one out of my former friends.

I liked reading your book, you seem tender. As I decisively leave femininity for a more masc appearance, I'm left thinking about who I'll be. Jess Goldberg was only one role model for people who look like me, felt like me, love like me. I guess I have two now, if you don't mind the openness. I want to be loving, gentle, tender. I see so much toxic and aggressive masculinity. The idea of becoming that scares me.

I thought about being an electrician. Life got in the way, I'm in school for nursing now. I don't know if you still feel this way, but being surrounded by feminine cis het women overwhelms me. I feel like I'm looking at who I was supposed to be. Does that go away with time, with a transition where people stop seeing you as a woman?

I have to apologize, I didn't have direction in this email. I never do. But I'm starting to realize if I let a lack of direction stop me from writing, I'll never write anything.

I hope your dog is well. I hope the pandemic is treating you well. I hope you're finding love. I hope the gigs haven't dried up too bad, I know a lot of my writer friends' have. I hope my rambling is at least entertaining.

With love and compassion,
Adonastare

OCTOBER 15, 2020

Dear Adonastare:

Thank you for your letter. It's very true, I do love letters, and I really loved yours.

I remember the very first time I picked up *Stone Butch Blues*. I look back on that day now as the fulcrum that it was, tipping me towards my future self. I was in the stuffy little space that was the old Little Sister's bookstore on Thurlow just off Davie Street in Vancouver, standing in front of a floor-to-ceiling bookshelf at the top of a narrow and well-worn staircase. Some memories soften with time, and their edges begin to bleed into other days or spaces inside your head. Other moments snap to attention and the details stiffen and solidify in your mind, everything in full colour and sharp focus. I was 23 years old. My second-hand black boots were two sizes too big for me. I had recently been given my very first necktie but no one had ever showed me how to tie it and there was no internet yet, no Google to ask. It was early September but still summer-hot, and I was sweating under a sports bra and tshirt and denim jacket. Most of me almost always covered by clothing not measured or stitched for me. Shoulders too wide, sleeves too long, loose at the neck, leaving me always unhemmed and itching inside my ill-fitting armour.

I was a small-town northern-Canadian kid raised by the 70s reading about a big-city factory-working butch forged in the filth and the grit of America in the 50s, but still I recognized the possibility of me in those pages. My foremotherfather. I flipped to the back of the book and saw a steel-jawed and determined older version of a face very much like mine staring back at me from the author's photo. Leslie

Feinberg was a real person, who had invented Jess to tell us that we had a history, that the past belonged partly to us, too. That we existed. There was a story out there that we were living in the centre of, not the victim, not the punchline, but the one who survived and wrote it all down. The storyteller.

I bought the book, brought it home, cried, and immediately read it four more times. I had yet to consciously seek out, or even mouth the words queer elder yet, but, looking back now, I realize I did have two or three or four, and had met and lost more than a handful already. But most of my elders did not look like me, did not dress like me. None of them ever told me a story that slipped easily on and fit my shoulders just right.

That was nearly thirty years ago.

The reason that I say the word elder with melancholy in my mouth is that even saying the word reminds me of who is missing, who we have lost, which one of us will not be in next year's family photo. When I say the word elder I know in my bones it is still too soon for it to belong to me, I have not learned enough yet, that someone left town without writing down the password, giving me the keys and telling me where the maps are kept. I can't make my mouth make the shape of the word elder without my tongue metaphorically travelling to a missing tooth in my head, a chipped incisor, a broken place, an aching cavity where it always hurts when I chew anything.

Sometimes elder only means that I am older than you, not that I feel aged or wise enough yet to deserve the title.

Like you said, given a few more decades, I won't have to describe to you how this moniker is both a reluctant honour, and a terrifying burden, pinned directly to my now-flat and tender chest, one I will do my best to earn and then earn again, every day. Leslie Feinberg died on November 15,

2014. I found out that my elder had passed by receiving an email from a reporter, asking me for a quote about how this made me feel.

I turned 51 years old this summer. Until the pandemic stopped the wheels constantly rolling under my life, I spent much of the year for most of the last nearly two decades on the road for work, touring festivals and conferences and schools, telling stories and doing shows. Since early March I have spent almost every minute of most hours under this same roof, or in our small backyard, bare feet on the grass and hands in the dirt, staring up at a now very familiar sky.

I did not realize until several months into sheltering at home just how deeply exhausted I was. How much I had normalized jet lag and gotten used to my heart pumping empty blood back into my veins. How much I needed to sit down in one spot and just think. How much I needed this time to consider, compare, catch up, collect my thoughts. Consciously determine and decide my next moves, not have them dictated to me by a calendar or commitments.

When I was a child I felt that all things feminine were forced upon me. My clothes and toys and walls were painted pale pink and yellow without my consent, my assigned sex decided how I was expected to talk and walk and laugh and play and think and love. I bucked and rebuked and forsook almost anything the world had labelled as inherently belonging to girls and women, in order to find some semblance of myself among all those expectations, all those rules written and assumed and enforced by the extremely binary world around me.

Only in the last few years have I learned to see how lucky I was to not ever be fully able to leave behind my tenderness, my tears. I am just now rediscovering the pieces of me I denied or covered with three layers of clothes, the soft and secret places that have always lived inside of me, but I mostly only revealed in whispers to lovers under covers in the night.

I think a storyteller who has lost their tenderness could only really be called a historian, so I am grateful now that I could never rid myself of mine.

You might not want to hear this, but fifty-something me is also left thinking of who I want to be when I grow up. I spend a lot of time these days delicately tinkering with my take on my own masculinity. I don't remember the first time I looked around and realized I was the oldest one in the room. I still remember thinking I would finally feel fully formed at forty, and then I got there and found I was still stumbling around on unsteady feet, unsure of which words fit me and what it meant to be trans but not trans enough, to be not quite a man, but never really a woman either.

Is this the part of this letter where I tell you I still find myself surrounded by a world that is constantly screaming in my ear that I am decidedly not who and what I was supposed to be?

The good news is, I have found the volume knob and turned it almost all the way off. Time has blessed me with caring so much less about the cisgender sea we all have to emerge out of to become ourselves. I no longer bother myself much with wondering if people see me as a woman or not, and that is the real transition I seek now. To become someone who lives authentically and with no regard for stereotypes. I am learning to revel and rejoice in my abject failure to conform to anyone's gender boxes, even the makeshift and improvised ones I assembled and constructed around a younger me to protect myself enough for me to make it to today.

I'm reading every essay and article and book I can find about toxic masculinity, and thinking about how to build and embody a better masculine being in this deeply misogynist society and world.

I'm realizing in order to really do this I have to dismantle the reluctant woman inside of me every bit as much as I need to rethink what we were all taught to believe a real man looks like. This to me is the grand gift that trans people have always brought into the light, the joyous and immensely painful labour we have endured in order to bring our offerings into this world. To reveal and resist this ancient lie that any of us can be simply defined by or refined down to our genitals, or our chromosomes. The fact that we have always existed, and every effort to extinguish, deny or erase us is just more proof of that. We are the only evidence we have ever needed.

I am learning to find comfort in the fact that one day I will have lived long enough to become old-fashioned, that my words and books and stories will only be dusted off and read to remind ourselves of a time when trans people still had to battle for our rights, for the ability to thrive and love and be celebrated. I continue to fight for the day when we don't have to fight anymore.

The dog is asleep on the little rug on the floor next to my desk. I can hear my love Sarah downstairs right now as she moves about the kitchen, heating up the leftovers from the dinner I made last night. I hope my ramblings find you well, and safe, and deeply loved somewhere tonight.

Stay tender, my Alaskan friend. Stay true. And please, stay in touch.

with love and hope,
Ivan

21.

BACK HOME

Ivan

Hello my friend. It's funny, when I read these words, even as I write them with my own hand, I hear them in your voice. I don't know if I've ever told you this, but aside from my mother, you're the only person I speak to on the phone. Despite the fact that I, an adult walking the fine line between a millennial and a gen Xer, have lost all interest in talking on the phone. But I still love when I see your name pop up on my screen.

I know you as someone that also likes to communicate by letter and email. I think there's something to be said for storytellers when they get the chance to really lean into the lost art of writing a letter, properly formed with a clear introduction, a thesis statement and thoughtful sign-off. You've told me about correspondence you've received over the years from people at speaking gigs, fans of your books and your voice and your you. One thing I know I've mentioned to you in one of our phone calls is how I have long wished I would have written you one. So consider this making up for lost time.

You see, I had this letter planned out, after a reading and q&a you did at the Kwanlin Dün Cultural Centre in Whitehorse a few years back. I wrote this letter in my head walking back to my apartment, up Black Street in the dusk of a Yukon night. How I wish I would have stuck around to meet you, shake your hand, and say thank you. Tell you how much it meant to see someone like me stand on a stage and talk and be joyful but emotional, strong and serious and funny. How much it meant to see a trans person made tangible in a place where it felt like an anomaly. I was in those early awkward stages of being out, to most of the people in that room it looked like I had just shaved the beard that lived on my face for 15 years, but to me and my heart I knew that my relationship to these people and my home was changing forever. That I was changing forever. This was a scary time in my life, we're both from the same town, the same streets and faces and we both know how it feels to challenge the expectations of who we are as Yukoners. I was scared, of myself, of my neighbours and friends, but most selfishly for myself.

It filled me with calm to watch you on that stage, to listen to you tell the stories of the life you have lived and the times that have challenged you and the perseverance you found. There's power in seeing someone not unlike yourself speak to the potential future of your experience. I wasn't sure what was ahead of me, but when I heard you speak, I wasn't afraid anymore. I could start to draw the map in my head of the route to discovering who I really was, under the matte finish of the "male" presentation I was hiding under.

I never did meet you that day, I was too scared to say hi and acknowledge how real this all felt, but we met shortly thereafter. I still remember going on drives with you, sitting in the passenger seat of a Nissan Pathfinder, looking out over the roofs of a city I knew I was leaving forever, the sky pink and blue and white, a fortuitous colour scheme. You would offer guidance and wisdom for the road ahead, as if you were packing me an emotional bug-out bag for my journey.

I still carry that bag with me and the idea of writing you this letter still feels difficult. Not because it's challenging but because it's hard to condense down just how much it's meant to me as a trans person that grew up in the Yukon to be connected to another. It's been the greatest joy in my life to know that there is always at least one person that understands both where I came from and also where I'm going.

Thank you for your words, your voice and your you.

Love
Niko

SEPTEMBER 19, 2020

Dearest Niko:

I read your email last night, after a long and exhausting day, and I had
to struggle with my urge to pick up the phone and press your number,
as I firmly believe that the honour of receiving a letter from a friend
calls for sitting down and answering with something tangible, something that can be read and read again, and saved. I love to hear a voice
on the phone, you know I do, especially these days, but a phone call is
fleeting, and it becomes a memory as soon as it is over, while a good letter can become a keepsake, an artifact.

Listen to me go on! Next I will be investing in a pot of ink and a
feather pen and red sealing wax. Jesus. I wish you had met my grandmother Patricia before she died. Now that woman could write a god-
damned letter.

I didn't know until you told me that you were at that gig at the
Kwanlin Dün that night. June 2018, I think it was. I really love that
space, I love that when they leave the back doors of the hall open you
can smell the pine logs burning in the firepit outside, I love that you can
see and feel the current of the mighty Yukon River moving right beside
us, I love that I can look across the water and see the hospital where I
was born squatting in the trees that cover the foothills of the mountain.

I remember my cousin Dan calling me up earlier that summer to tell
me that he had this friend I had to meet, that you had just come out as
trans, that there was now another trans person in town who was from
the Yukon, like really another trans Yukoner, not someone who had
just moved up from a big city down south, but someone who knew.
Someone who knew all the back roads, and the secret party spots, and
who had lived through F.H. Collins Secondary School and only bought

their coffee from Midnight Sun, never that place on Main St., and who remembered what used to be where the Walmart is now, and what the waterfront looked like before those condos were built, and whose mom knew my mom. My dad bought all the glass for his house from your dad. You know what I mean. Someone who had always had a block heater installed in their vehicle, even the beaters. Someone who knows the smell of pine sap in July, and the taste of frozen over the winter cranberries when the snow first melts, and loves 11 a.m. winter sunrises like I do.

The other thing I remember about that night, that night we never quite met, was that was the night that my old guidance counsellor introduced me, and fumbled around so much with my pronouns, which was awkward for everyone as the gig was sponsored by the Yukon Human Rights Commission, right? And anyways, of course good old high school came up, and that is when someone from the audience shouted out did I know that the old FH was on fire? I knew the building itself had been torn down a few weeks prior, I had seen the article in the *Yukon News* that showed the hazmat teams in white coveralls and masks sifting through the rubble in front of a row of bulldozers and backhoes, a powdery cloud of asbestos and drywall dust looming in the air. What I didn't know until that night was that they trucked those dump trucks full of scrap wood and ancient floor tiles and crumbled concrete blocks up to the dump, and backfilled over it all, but that the remains of our old high school had ignited somehow, causing a giant underground toxic dumpster fire to burn for over a month before it could be formally and finally extinguished. Something both of us would have agreed was both environmentally concerning, and metaphorically and poetically on point, had we met that night.

I remember when we first started hanging out, drinking too much coffee and borrowing my mom's truck to drive up to the Grey Mountain lookout and talk, I would have these almost overwhelming waves of emotion build in my chest and then burst and race down into my gut, and up towards the crown of my head, and out to my fingertips. A hot and chaotic wave, running around and kicking inside of me with no real means of escape. This strange mix of feelings would gather and pool behind my eyes, kind of pressurized. It's hard to describe. I would sit in the driver's seat and listen to you talk, your profile edged by sunrise, the sky a wash of cool pink and blue northern light, the truck smelling like coffee and wet wool mittens, and I would feel fiercely protective of you. Fear and hope and love and joy and anger would all fight in my throat. It was like in my heart I knew our hometown, stretched out below us on the other side of that cracked windshield, was going to come for you, and I would never really be able to position myself directly in front of you and fend it off, I would only ever be able to stand behind you, or beside you, at very best. I knew even in that moment the most I could ever do would be to be there for you to lean on, or maybe to catch you if you fell back when it inevitably happened.

The Yukon makes all kinds of space for women to connect with their masculine selves, and in some ways the celebration of axe-wielding tire-changing self-sufficient northern women had offered me a buffer, a bit of a forcefield, as younger me stumbled into and found my butch self, and later, stretched and grew into my trans and non-binary skin.

I knew it would be much different for you, shedding your beard and standing up and being seen as your transfeminine self.

I don't blame you for leaving. When you told me you were moving to Toronto, your words travelled right out of the speaker in my cell phone and directly into to my eighteen-year-old baby butch spine. I will never forgive our hometown for raising the asshole who snuck up behind you and sucker-punched you that night right outside of your apartment. I know we still don't know who he was, and probably never will, but in my heart I believe that he probably once walked the halls of F.H. Collins, just like we did. I know he was not a stranger, and that truth slays me, it truly does. I hate that you felt like you had to leave, but I get it, I do.

I remember when I left for real the first time. Packing all my stuff into that shitbox of a van and steering due south, alone with the stereo cranked and Alaska Highway dust in my teeth. I knew that place couldn't change fast enough to keep up with who I needed to become. I knew I could not unravel myself with all of my history gathered around me repeating over and over who I used to be, who I was supposed to be. Pat's daughter. Dan's cousin. Florence's oldest grandchild. Carrie's big sister.

But I didn't leave town with a black eye like you did. I will never ever forget that reality.

Last night when I was reading your email again, I couldn't stop thinking about that time we all went to the hot springs, I think it was January 2019?

I remember all five of us entering the women's change room, and you and I both falling very silent. Slipping out of our parkas and snow boots and quickly donning bathing suits, in the very last stretch of benches by the door that led to the pool. I was mostly staring at the floor, like I always do, heart pounding just a little, like it always is. I glanced up to check in on you, and our eyes met.

I cannot even say how much I loved you in that moment, cannot describe the immense relief, the giant fifty-year-old breath I exhaled into the small space between us. Two of us, with backup. Knowing that if anyone fucked with us that night, in the change rooms or in the pool, that we had each other, and Inga, and Antoinette and Sarah, too. Two Yukoners, a German, a Tobagonian-Torontonian, and a Swede. I felt like

I had a giant fanged and clawed mother grizzly bear living just under my tender skin, and we would both be safe. We were all safe. For the first time, I think maybe ever in my life, I changed into my swimsuit in a public pool completely unafraid.

Remember that morning I tried telling you in my mom's truck up on Grey Mountain that the big-city trans community might not be the welcoming, accepting, blissful soft landing that I would like it to be for you? You sipped your oat milk latte and nodded, but I could tell that in your head you were patting me on the shoulder and saying ok Uncle Ivan, ok old fella, I'm listening, but I know it will be different for me.

I so wish it had been different for you. I wish trans people could come together better, that our own pain and trauma didn't get in the way so much. I wish we could trust one another more, forgive each other easier, welcome and hold and teach each other, without punishing those of us who are newer, or older, or younger, or who arrive on our doorsteps without the right words, or clothes, or politics. I wish we didn't turn so much of the hate aimed at us inward, and flip and bite our brothers and sisters and siblings simply because of their proximity, because they are available, and because they are so much easier to sink our teeth into than our real enemies are. They call it lateral violence, which is a useful term to a point, but one that does not fully describe how we can also harm those above us, and especially under us, and who arrive after us, and who we were meant to follow as well, not just those directly next to, or around us. I wish we had the same patience and compassion for each other that we muster up on the regular and extend to our families, our co-workers, to some confused stranger in a public bathroom at the mall.

We are so used to being given nothing, that we do not yet know how to gracefully inherit anything, and some of us are terrified that if we share what we have fought for and earned, that we will be left without enough.

The lesson I take from this is to make room for each and every one of us to bring ourselves, imperfect and carrying our mistakes still on our backs, into the change room. It is the only way forward I can see myself walking towards.

I want you to know how much your friendship means to me. How much I cherish our shared history, the common dirt caught in the treads in our boots. I have watched you grow your bangs out, and stretch and become your true and beautiful self over these last few years with such pride and hope for you.

I have found so much comfort and solace in the friendship and trust that we have built between us over the last three years, and learned a lot from standing next to you, fangs and claws hidden, but always ready. I hope we get to watch each other grow very old. I hope we mend many tears together, and shed many tears, and laugh until we pee our snow pants a little.

I hope one day we are both able to forgive Whitehorse and drive up Grey Mountain and park at the first lookout, by the graveyard there, and stare down at all those roofs, and those thin straws of woodsmoke reaching up into the sky, and marvel at how much everything has changed, and how good it feels to come home.

I know I've said this over the phone to you more than once, but here it is, on the page, and in the official archive: I am grateful to count you as family.

With much love,
Ivan

ACKNOWLEDGEMENTS

While it is always true that behind every book is a team of people whose work and love and attention should be sincerely thanked and acknowledged, this is especially and poignantly true for this book. Make yourself a coffee and sit down, because this is going to take a while.

I must first thank each and every person who wrote one of the letters that make up the backbone and foundations of this book. I am deeply honoured and grateful for each and every one of the voices and lives that appear in these pages. Some of their names have been changed to keep them safe or protect their privacy, but may every one of them see their name or pseudonym and know that my gratitude is the real deal: Ace Gregory Amundson (Sam), Ayesha Ali, Victoria Grey, Niko Stratis, Darach Seaton, Gord Dickson, Finn Dickson, Cal, Dianne J, Robert L, and Aiden C, fogel fogel, Ferron, Syd Lapan, Lynne T, Kate Lightstone, Adonastare Desmynier, Adri Kroll, Kate Kroll, Lee Harper, Atticus Harper, Leslee, Tem McCutcheon, Connor

Alan Phillips, Melinda Roy, Angela Bailly, Lys Morton, and last, the mysterious and as of yet unidentified note-leaver, S. S., if you read this, please be in touch with me, I have two free copies of this book and a cheque for you.

I also want to thank everyone who ever wrote me a letter that is still sitting in my desk or in my "special letter" file in my email inbox, awaiting a deserved response. It is not possible to include all of them here, but please know that every special letter I've ever received was at least in part in my heart when I sat down to connect all the dots and construct this book, this beautiful back and forth conversation of souls and stories and struggle and joy and hope that has been collected in these pages. This book has reminded me of something my grandmother Patricia always knew and taught me from an early age: the importance of letters. Sacred and tangible and physical correspondence. I hope reading this book encourages us all to find the good stationary, and buy a new pen, and sit down and write that letter we have been meaning to for years.

The pandemic and circumstance and work has separated me temporarily from most of my belongings, including a box of my grandmother's correspondence that she tucked away at various points in her 98 years of life. I hereby promise to read through them all again when life permits me to, and to learn and remember them better.

I also need to thank Jared Bland at McClelland and Stewart, who, even while trying to steer a publishing house through a pandemic, still took the time to call me once a week for six months and talk for at least an hour about this book, about its direction and progress and spirit and intentions. I not only gained an editor in this process, together we grew a whole big and wide and beautiful friendship. Also from McClelland and Stewart, I must thank Kimberlee Hesas, managing editor, Ruta

Liormonas, my pandemic-savvy publicist, Erin Kelly in the marketing department, and Sarah Howland in sales.

Because this book contains the private correspondence of real people, this manuscript has been through multiple drafts, and many little changes have been made along the way to respect the wishes and privacy and sometimes safety of the letter writers, which means that every care and precaution had to be taken at many steps to ensure we made as few mistakes as was possible in this process. Steady, careful and sharp eyes were required to make this happen, so I must thank copyeditor Melanie Little, and Jazz Cook for their loving proofread.

I also want to thank Kate Sinclair for her cover design, and for allowing me to take a picture of the ceiling of the room I wrote this book in, illuminated by a light I bought from an ad on Instagram, which magically calls to my mind both the northern lights and swimming up towards the sun at the same time, and using that as the inspiration for this cover. To anyone picking up this book the dustjacket might appear to be a blue and green and pink abstract design on a piece of paper, but to me it sings about my forever home, the north, and the feeling of swimming naked and unencumbered by clothes or shame or labels, with a little nod to the trans flag tossed in as cream cheese icing on top.

My eternal and deep gratitude to my agent Rachel Letofsky and the entire team at CookeMcDermid. Rachel, I have learned to see you as my big sister in this new publishing journey we have embarked upon, even though I've never asked and I'm pretty sure you are younger than me. I love having you in my corner, and I am sincerely thankful to be guided by your wisdom and love of writers and books and smashing the patriarchy.

I would also like to thank the Canada Council for the Arts for their kind support of this project, on behalf of both myself, and of the letter writers as well. My eternal gratitude to the University of Western Ontario, for making me the Alice Munro Chair in Creativity in the early days of the pandemic, thus allowing me the time and focus to complete this manuscript in what for me was a very short period of time.

I must pause and make space to thank Arsenal Pulp Press, especially Brian Lam, Robert Ballantyne, Cynara Geissler, Shirarose Wilensky, and all the folks I worked with there over the last 23 years. Arsenal Pulp Press is and always will be my publishing family, and I thank you for our continued relationship and support of me, even as I move forward and explore new relationships and possibilities. You believed in me first and you helped make me, and I continue to be fiercely proud of our history and the books you continue to champion and bring into this world.

I wrote the lion's share of my parts of this book from April through September of 2020. It was an intense process that required both me and the other letter writers to revisit some painful places, and to truly investigate the attics and basements of what we mean when we use words like compassion, and forgiveness, and repair. I must acknowledge the kind and open ears and thoughtful feedback that Niko Stratis, barbara findlay, and Carly Boyce gifted me with during this time. I will never forget your help, and I hope to be offered a chance to return it at some point in our futures.

I want to thank the creators of the music I listened to while I was writing this book. Many of them I am lucky enough to know a little, and some I am blessed enough to call friends, which is another gift that touring and performing has brought to me. They cannot all be named here for fear of missing somebody, but I think it deserves mentioning how much their music and lyrics inspired and moved me to continue writing through tears, and complicated memories, and the merciless stream of bad news going on in the world on the other side of the window. This book would not exist without your music.

I want to thank every member of my family, especially my mom Patricia, my sister Carrie, my father Donald, my Aunt Roberta, my Uncle Rob, my Uncle Fred, and my cousin Dan and his wife Sarah, for their decades now of help and support that always stands just off camera on the metaphorical stage in these pages. Some of the words in this book were painful for me to compose and record, but I was faithfully guided by my unconditional and eternal love for all of you as I wrote. As always, I hope that my writing honours you, even marginally more than it embarrasses you, or makes you want to scream "but that's not exactly how it happened!!!" Anyone who knows me knows how much I love my entire giant, complicated, opinionated and beautiful family. Any errors in these pages are mine and mine alone, and I cannot wait until we can all gather together safely again and constantly interrupt each other like we do and you can tell me exactly where I got it all wrong. I miss you all more than I ever thought I would, or could, or should.

This is where I thank my other family, brought into my life by my partner and collaborator and co-conspirator and daily inspiration Sarah MacDougall. Sarah, I know I tell you every day, even when you are watching sound engineering videos on your phone at lunch and are not even listening, but I love you so much and I can't think of anyone else I would rather live through a pandemic with. Your dedication to art and music and the creative life keeps my heart beating and my brain imagining and my fingers typing, even on these grey and frozen days of late January. I can't wait to watch the spring return to the little bit of dirt outside our window. Thank you for bringing your father Van, and his partner Lorie, and your sister Anna and her family, and your mom

Ann-Britt, and our dog Lucky into my world. Their love is your love is my love, and I return it like it was running in my veins. I also want to thank Sarah's grandmother Kitty, for her almost bottomless supply of Zip-locks, dishwasher pellets and parchment paper that she left us, and for the four solid walls and the roof I was protected by and kept warm inside of as I wrote these words.

Lastly, I thank my grandmothers Florence Amelia Mary Daws and Patricia Rita Cumming. Not a day goes by that I don't miss you both, and try to make decisions and fix my mistakes and keep my promises and save my money and live my life in a way that would make you both proud of me.

ABOUT THE AUTHOR

Ivan Coyote is a writer and storyteller. Born and raised in Whitehorse, Yukon, they are the author of thirteen books, the creator of four films, six stage shows, and three albums that combine storytelling with music. Coyote's books have won the ReLit Award, been named a Stonewall Honor Book, been longlisted for Canada Reads, shortlisted for the Hilary Weston Writers' Trust Prize for Nonfiction, and awarded the BC and Yukon Book Prizes' inaugural Jim Deva Prize for Writing That Provokes. In 2017, Ivan was given an honorary Doctor of Laws from Simon Fraser University for their writing and activism.